THE AQUARIUM
The Man in the Green Muffler
& I Didn't Always Live Here

PLAYSCRIPT 74

The Aquarium

The Man in the Green Muffler

& I Didn't Always Live Here

Stewart Conn

JOHN CALDER · LONDON

First published in Great Britain in 1976
by John Calder (Publishers) Ltd.
18 Brewer Street London W1R 4AS

© Stewart Conn 1976

All performing rights in these plays are strictly reserved and
applications for performances should be made to

Harvey Unna and Stephen Durbridge Ltd
14 Beaumont Mews
Marylebone High Street
London W1N 4HE

No performances of the plays may be given unless a licence
has been obtained prior to rehearsal

ALL RIGHTS RESERVED

ISBN 0 7145 3524 9 Casebound

Any paperback edition of this book whether published
simultaneously with, or subsequent to, the cased edition is
sold subject to the condition that it shall not, by way of
trade, be lent, resold, hired out, or otherwise disposed of,
without the publishers' consent, in any form of binding or
cover other than that in which it is published.

All rights reserved. No part of this publication may be
reproduced, stored in a retrieval system, or transmitted
by any form or by any means, electronic, mechanical,
photocopying, recording or otherwise, without the prior
written permission of the copyright owner.

Typesetting by Gilbert Composing Services, Leighton Buzzard
Printed by Thomson Litho Ltd., East Kilbride, Scotland

CONTENTS

PREFACE

I Didn't Always Live Here was first presented in the Glasgow Citizens' Theatre, and *The Aquarium* by the Royal Lyceum Company of Edinburgh. Both plays, extensively revised, were subsequently performed within a few months of one another by the Dundee Repertory Company. The director in each case was Stephen MacDonald, to whom I acknowledge a particular debt of gratitude.

INTRODUCTION

The Aquarium, perhaps surprisingly, uses a naturalistic
format. The term could, however, be misleading, if
treated as more than a stepping-stone to the play's
actual intentions.

The word poetic has its own dangers, even when it is
used to denote not overt poeticism or symbolism but
resonance and, ideally, illumination. Suffice it to say
that *The Aquarium* is essentially theatrical. This theatri-
cality must be allowed to express itself, and not be stifled
by over-attention to functional detail. In particular the
world outside should be conjured up not by elaborate
pauses and sound-effects, but through sensitivity towards
the play's rhythms and changes of mood.

One limitation of naturalism is that of expectancy. I
have tried, within the play's accepted framework, to
cater for colour and surprise. A way of obtaining this, in
performance, is by imaginative use of lighting and
lighting-sources. This is especially true of the final scene:
TOM's fantasy must be heightened yet remain real, which
it is; and careful changes in emotional temperature are
essential in the section which follows and when ELLA
appears.

Without her realising it ELLA cuts critically across,
and transforms, the main action. Through her the world
onstage and the world offstage meet; the one, as though
by remote control, influencing the other. It should be as
though she were delivering the clinching couplet of a
sonnet, revealing that the rest has rhymed. Only then will
the ending come across with the required impact and
dramatic inevitability. Only then can the characters
inhabit the audience's imagination, which is where they
belong.

The Man in the Green Muffler is a short conversation
piece. Its climax relates a simple visual image to under-
currents in the preceding dialogue. I hope the writing
works both on an obvious surface level= and on that of
analogy.

I Didn't Always Live Here, the other full-length play in
the volume, has been called 'a hymn to Glasgow'. The
writing certainly stems less from first-hand experience
than from impressions and, I suppose, affection. This

9

might be reflected in any production of the play: in modulation of tone, and a care that the actors are not impeded or dominated by too literal a set.

Three distinct playing areas are needed. MARTHA's room occupies the major portion of the stage. It has a door to the stairhead, a curtained exit to the kitchen, and an internal staircase to the attic—a makeshift space cut in the joists, with a skylight providing access to the roof. The remainder of the stage is taken up by AMIE's slightly better furnished room; again with one exit to the kitchen and another to (as she prefers to call it) the landing.

It is of course MARTHA's play. She lives with her budgie, in the crumbling tenement. And flashbacks show moments from her past—in the years of the Depression, the Blitz, and shortly after the War. But sympathy extends also to AMIE, her isolation if anything the more pitiable for being self-imposed; to MacWHURRIE with his dilemma of faith; and to JACK, the ghost from MARTHA's past, as he succumbs to grief.

Audience response for this play has been more heartwarming than for anything else I've written. It may be that its blend of tears and laughter is better (or more fortuitously) managed, than in any of my other plays. At the same time I like to think something of its human values got across.

Whatever class the characters in *The Aquarium* and *I Didn't Always Live Here* belong to, and whatever attitudes they appear to depict, they are first and fore-most human beings—with private lives, longings and terrors, as well as a social function. And the area with which I'm primarily concerned, no matter what the accent or environment of any one character, is that of the heart.

I find the line between pessimism and optimism no easier in writing, than in life. With relief, on rereading these plays, I detect at least the hope that however bleak the prospect, and the individual odds against, *all* may not ultimately be lost.

Stewart Conn
Glasgow

THE AQUARIUM

A Play in Two Acts

The Aquarium was first performed by the Royal Lyceum Company of Edinburgh on 8th May 1973, with the following cast:

HARRY RANKIN	Callum Mill
EDITH, his wife	Geraldine Newman
TOM, their son	Paul Young
ELLA	Eileen McCallum

The play was directed by Bill Bryden.

This two act version was presented by the Dundee Repertory Company on 19th September 1973, with the following cast:

HARRY	Andrew Crawford
EDITH	Ursula Smith
TOM	Tom Cotcher
ELLA	Janet Michael

The play was directed by Stephen MacDonald.

ACT ONE

Scene 1

The living room. Two doors: one to the kitchen, the other to the hall and the rest of the flat. An elaborate cornice, broken along one wall by a room-division. A service-hatch. A sideboard: on it, a small brass bell. A table, chairs, bookcase. A long sofa. Near it, a standard lamp. On the mantel piece, a small silver cup. Over it, a mirror. Pot-plants. Downstage, an electric radiator. Upstage, a grandfather clock.

From the wide bay window, with its net curtains, would be seen the stonework and roofs of tenement or terrace houses, glimpsed through (or over) trees.

The stage is empty.

HARRY. *(Off)* Blast!

> *(HARRY enters. His face is half-lathered and he carries a razor, a shaving-mirror, a towel and a facecloth. He lays these on the sideboard, goes to the kitchen.)*

One damn thing after another. . .

(He returns with a bowl of water, puts it down. He listens a moment, crosses to the grandfather clock, cautiously opens the front, and brings out a full half-bottle of whisky. He opens it, fills the cap, drinks—and does the same again. He replaces the bottle. As he closes the front of the clock, it starts striking. He looks at it.

The front door slams, off. HARRY moves back, sits.

TOM enters, carrying a cardboard toilet-roll box heaped with groceries. He lays it on the hatch. The clock is still striking.

13

TOM *takes off his coat, is about to sling it over a chair. They exchange a look. On his way to the hall, to hang up his coat,* TOM *gives the clock a hefty thump. It stops striking.)*

What was that for?

TOM.   What?

HARRY.   No need for that.

(TOM *exits to the hall.)*

TOM.   *(Off)* Stopped, hasn't it? What more do you want?

HARRY.   Damage the works. How often do you have to be told?

(TOM *comes in, without his coat.)*

TOM.   What were you trying to do, hypnotise it?

HARRY.   I was counting the strikes.

TOM.   That's a useful activity. Really purposeful. If we were all to do that, couple of hours a day, six days a week, we'd have the country on its feet in no time.

HARRY.   It's a question. . . of balance. . . They're finely balanced.

(TOM *has gone to the kitchen. He takes packages from the grocery box.)*

TOM.   *(Off)* Anyway, I thought you'd stopped it.

HARRY.   So I had.

TOM.   *(Off)* Didn't make a very good job of it.

HARRY.   What could have started it?

TOM.   *(Off)* You prancing around, I suppose. *(Reappears at the hatch)* Maybe it was one of Frank's vibrations.

(HARRY *is shaving.* TOM *takes the remaining groceries from the box. Something falls, in the kitchen.)*

HARRY.   I hope that's not the eggs.

TOM.   *(Off)* No such luck.

(TOM *comes in, sits and starts reading a magazine.)*

14

HARRY. Are you ready?

TOM. Look who's talking!

(HARRY *stops shaving.*)

HARRY. Did you try starting the car?

TOM. It'll be okay.

HARRY. How do you know? In this weather? All this condensation?

TOM. We can always get a taxi.

HARRY. Have you packed her things?

TOM. What do you think I am, a yo-yo? What'll I take?

HARRY. Whatever you think she'll need.

(TOM *rises.* HARRY *continues shaving.*)

TOM. Good job I didn't bump into Ella on the stairs. She'd have thought we'd all gone down with dysentry. *(He exits. Off)* Why aren't you shaving in the bathroom?

HARRY. *(Calls)* What?

TOM. *(Off)* Don't you usually shave in the bathroom?

HARRY. The bulb's gone.

(Pause.

TOM *enters, carrying a slip, a brassiere and a pair of tights. He holds the brassiere in front of his chest.* HARRY *sees him in the mirror, glares, and goes back to his shaving.*

TOM *lays the clothes on the divan.)*

(Suddenly) Bloody hell!

TOM. Cut yourself?

HARRY. Get my styptic.

(TOM *exits.* HARRY *dabs his chin.* TOM *comes in with a bottle which he opens and hands to* HARRY.)

TOM. Couldn't find it. Here's my Old Spice.

HARRY. *(Sniffs it)* Smells like a pooves' picnic.

TOM. Wouldn't know. I've never been to one.

(HARRY *applies the lotion.*)

Stings, does it?

HARRY.   What do you think?

(TOM *examines the cut.*)

TOM.   You must have nicked a bit clean out.

HARRY.   It's still bleeding.

TOM.   Maybe it's an artery.

(TOM *gets a toilet-roll from among the groceries, opens it and tears off a small piece of toilet-paper which* HARRY *puts on the cut.*)

HARRY.   Thanks.

TOM.   So long as the blade isn't rusty. Or you might get lockjaw. *(Turning away)* Beats me why you don't go electric.

(TOM *exits.*

HARRY *rubs his face with the damp cloth, picks up the bowl and heads for the kitchen.*)

HARRY.   *(Calls)* Better bring her coat. For warmth.

TOM.   *(Off)* Her plastic mac?

HARRY.   *(Off)* Her heavy coat.

TOM.   *(Off)* Where is it?

(Pause.)

HARRY.   *(Comes in from the kitchen)* And a cardigan, when you're at it. *(Pause)* Did you hear me, Tom?

TOM.   *(Off)* All right, all right . . .

HARRY.   Never know . . . this weather . . . and the car's draughty . . . Wouldn't want her to catch her . . .

(HE *breaks off, as* TOM *comes in carrying a dress, plus coat and cardigan. Pause.*)

TOM.   Catch her what?

HARRY.   Catch a chill. We'll need something to put these in.

TOM.   Under the sink.

(Pause.)

16

HARRY. Fetch it, then. And what about shoes?

(TOM *sighs, lays the clothes down, exits.* HARRY *is cleaning his razor.* TOM *comes in with a tartan travelling grip, which he drops in front of* HARRY.)

This bag's filthy. What's been in it?

TOM. Potatoes.

HARRY. It's the bag I use for my golf things. Your mother knows that.

TOM. Here, use this *Herald.* Best place for it.

(TOM *picks up a* Glasgow Herald, *tosses it to* HARRY, *who stuffs it into the grip, then starts putting the clothes in.* TOM *exits.)*

TOM. *(Off)* You haven't set foot on a golf-course for years.

HARRY. Nothing to stop me taking it up again . . . Only stopped because old Bill popped it. Broke up our foursome. Come to think of it, I wouldn't mind . . . When the good weather comes in again . . . a few holes . . . *(Makes a few putting strokes)*

(TOM *comes in again, with shoes and a shoebrush.)*

TOM. Thought your lot just played the 19th eighteen times.

(TOM *has started to polish one of the shoes.)*

HARRY. These don't need polishing . . . they're clean.

TOM. That's because I'm polishing them. *(Puts one shoe in the grip, starts on the other)*

HARRY. You've crumpled her coat.

(HARRY *takes the coat, refolds it carefully but none too neatly, and replaces it in the grip.* TOM *is polishing the other shoe vigorously.)*

That'll do fine . . . Tom . . .

TOM. Just a minute.

HARRY. We haven't time.

(TOM *keeps polishing.)*

Put it in the bag.

(TOM *throws down the shoe and the brush.)*

17

TOM. Put it in the bag yourself. *(He exits)*

(HARRY puts the shoe in, and starts to zip the bag. The zip sticks. He tugs at it: still it catches.)

HARRY. Who the blazes invented zips!

(Doorbell rings, off.)

(Calls) Tom!

TOM. *(Off)* I'm in the bog.

(HARRY goes to answer. The bell rings again, breaking off as he reaches the front door.

The stage is empty. Voices, off. The front door closes, off.)

HARRY. *(Off)* Tom!

(Pause.

HARRY appears. He has a large bouquet of flowers, in cellophane and tied with a ribbon.

TOM comes in. He pretends he is a photographer, snapping HARRY from a variety of angles.)

TOM. Big smile, that's it . . . Click! And again . . . say cheese. . . Click! And now one for our sponsors . . . that's it . . . Click! Thank you. Give the gentleman a big hand. . .

HARRY. Who are they from?

(TOM removes an envelope from the flowers.)

TOM. Abracadabra! For my next trick . . . *(He brings out a card)*

HARRY. There isn't time to fool around.

TOM. *(Points at HARRY)* Didn't you know? And you were generous enough to include me in your magnanimous gesture.

HARRY. For crying out loud, they must have cost a . . .

(He breaks off as TOM looks at him.)

Not that I object, Tom. Under the circumstances. Your mother'll be delighted . . . They're very nice. . .

TOM. Sooner they're in water, the better.

(HARRY *goes to the kitchen.*

TOM *combs his hair, at the mirror.*)

HARRY. *(Off)* Pretty pricey, all the same. The delivery, I mean . . . Could we not have collected them?

TOM. Why not splash out, for once?

(HARRY *comes in from the kitchen.*)

HARRY. They're very pretty . . . brighten the place up for her.

TOM. It could do with it.

HARRY. It's no palace, I grant you.

TOM. Say that again.

HARRY. But it's good enough for your mother and me.

TOM. Could do with redecorating.

HARRY. What's stopping you?

TOM. I'd meant to start on my own room.

HARRY. Well?

TOM. No point putting up wallpaper, if there's damp underneath.

HARRY. Damp!

TOM. You can smell it. *(He sits, reads his magazine.)*

HARRY. You have to . . . accept a certain amount of dampness . . . in these old buildings, over eighty years old you know, Tom. . . They weren't built yesterday . . . I mean . . . it stands to reason, doesn't it? It can't be avoided.

TOM. Yes it can.

HARRY. How?

TOM. By having the place properly surveyed.

HARRY. I had it surveyed.

TOM. On the cheap.

HARRY. In business you have to take advantage of. . . professional contacts.

TOM. You mean they take advantage of you. Did they examine the roof?

HARRY. They told me there was nothing to worry about... unduly. Anyway, I haven't noticed it having any ill effects on you.

TOM. Me! I'm a classical case of environmental neurosis. The middle-class Glaswegian: a study in decay.

HARRY. Don't talk rot.

TOM. That's it. Rot! Wet rot, dry rot... we've got them all. We're hemmed in by it. Haven't you noticed? It's in the air we breathe ... spores ... in the atmosphere ...

HARRY. Your imagination's running riot.

TOM. There's no light, for a start.

HARRY. We face north, you fool.

(A moment's silence.)

TOM. Why are you wearing that tie?

HARRY. What's wrong with it?

TOM. It's black.

HARRY. Blue.

TOM. Black.

HARRY. It's navy. Navy blue.

TOM. Black.

HARRY. Blue.

TOM. Ballocks.

(Pause.)

Look, have you not something... well, a bit... less funereal?

(HARRY *looks at him.*)

Just a minute. *(He exits)*

(HARRY *crosses to the window, squints at his tie.)*

HARRY. *(To himself)* Navy blue!

(TOM *comes in, a selection of ties over one arm. He adopts a salesman manner.)*

TOM.   Now . . . what would Sir fancy? We used to do a
strong line in Scottish regiments, but fashions
change . . .

HARRY.   Come on, there isn't . . . *(He takes off his own
tie.)*

TOM.   Or a rejuvenated slimline, as sported by the late
Baillie Vass in person. No? Aaaah. . . Sir's taste
is impeccable!

(HARRY *has chosen the most muted tie. He puts
it on.)*

A pity about Sir's facial blemish.

HARRY.   Blast, I'd forgotten. *(He looks at his face in
the mirror, dabs the cut.)*

(TOM lays the ties on the divan.)

Must have been deep, right enough. You could
zip up that bag.

(TOM *stoops, zips the travelling grip in one easy
movement.* HARRY *appears momentarily non-
plussed, but says nothing.* TOM *looks up.*

HARRY *exits, throwing a look at the bag.)*

(Off) Oh . . . would you mind collecting my sports
jacket from the cleaners. Afterwards.

TOM.   Sure.

HARRY.   *(Off)* You won't forget? *(Comes in putting
his suit jacket on.)*

(TOM *holds out a hand.* HARRY *brings out his
wallet.)*

There. *(He gives* TOM *a pound note)* And here. . .
(Hands him another pound) For my share of the
flowers. . .

TOM.   Ta. *(He stuffs the notes in his hip pocket.)*

HARRY.   How often do I have to tell you, that's a
dangerous habit.

TOM.   Sure, Byres Road's hoaching with pickpockets.

HARRY.   You'll learn your lesson one of these days.

(TOM *exits, comes in again putting on his coat.)*

TOM. Look, Dad. . .

    (Pause.)

    You'll be careful, where Mum's concerned?

HARRY. I don't know what you mean.

TOM. Not to. . . to upset her. We must remember to act. . . as if everything were normal.

HARRY. She's in for a check-up. Routine check-up. Happens to hundreds of people, every day of the week. Purely as a precaution. A safety-measure. Nothing abnormal about it.

TOM. So long as you stick to that.

    (HARRY *frowns. Pause, then:)*

    One other thing, Dad. . . When they tell you, I don't want to be kept in the dark.

HARRY. There's nothing to worry about. Everything's going to be hunkey-dorey.

TOM. I hope so.

    (HARRY *exits.)*

HARRY. *(Off)* It won't be easy, for either of us.

TOM. Or for her.

    (HARRY *comes in, putting on his coat.)*

HARRY. Are you ready?

TOM. Got the keys?

HARRY. Yes. *(Taking the car keys from his pocket)* I know you think I. . . sometimes don't care. Maybe I sometimes don't seem to. But I do. I do, Tom. It's just that. . . whenever I try to show it. . .

    (TOM *takes the keys.)*

TOM. You don't have to. . . say anything.

    (HARRY *looks at him.)*

HARRY. On you go. . . I'll. . . be right down. . . I want to. . . find my gloves. . .

    (TOM *exits. As* HARRY *is crossing the room towards the clock,* TOM *reappears.)*

What now?

(Pause.)

TOM. *(Falsetto, American small boy voice)* Say Dad, that's the garbage-man at the door.

HARRY. *(Basso, American accent)* Tell him we don't want any!

(Pause. Then TOM *takes the bag, and exits.*

*(*HARRY *looks momentarily wistful, then his expression changes. He crosses to the clock, takes out the bottle, drinks. About to replace the bottle, he changes his mind. He looks around, crosses to the bookcase, puts the bottle behind some books. He returns to the clock, gingerly closes the front. It does not strike. He feels in his pockets, brings out his gloves. He exits. The front door closes, off.)*

Scene 2

As the lights come up, the stage is empty. Pause, then the door opens.

EDITH enters. She is younger than HARRY. She moves round the room, glances in the mirror, straightens an ornament, exmaines the plants.

Front door closes, off. HARRY comes in. He takes off his gloves, puts them in his coat pocket. As he steps forward:

EDITH. It's wonderful to be home, Harry.

HARRY. It's wonderful to have you back, Edith.

> *(She is centre stage. He takes her coat, exits with it, returns, having taken his own coat off.)*

EDITH. The clock's stopped.

HARRY. I stopped it. It was getting a bit much.

EDITH. What can I do?

HARRY. You can sit there, while I make you a cup of tea.

EDITH. There's no hurry, really. . . I had one before you came for me.

HARRY. I'll put the kettle on, anyway.

EDITH. I'll do it.

HARRY. Edith. . . you'll sit down. . . and relax. . . If you won't go to bed, the least you can do. . .

> *(He eases her into a chair.)*

EDITH. Everything's so tidy.

HARRY. You haven't seen in there! *(Indicates the kitchen)* or Tom's room.

EDITH. How did you and Tom. . . get on?

HARRY. Like a house on fire.

EDITH. Did you stick to the menus?

HARRY. Except for one night. And Ella kept us in soup.

EDITH. Bless her.

HARRY. Tureens of it. Blast, that reminds me.

24

(He crosses to the kitchen.)

EDITH. I hope you've been taking your pills, Harry.

HARRY. *(At the hatch)* Every day, without fail. Honest Injun. *(He brings the bouquet of flowers to her.)*

EDITH. How lovely. . . From you and Tom. . . It's far too generous of you both. Was it your idea?

HARRY. Tom's. But I paid my share.

EDITH. I didn't mean that.

(EDITH removes the flowers from their cellophane; and arranges them in the bowl.)

They're absolutely perfect. Thank you. *(She kisses him lightly.)*

HARRY. Is there. . . anything I can get you? Are you sure? You're not tired?

EDITH. I'm fine. . .

HARRY. Here, put your feet up. . .

(He removes TOM's ties from the sofa, and arranges a cushion for her. She settles. He stands watching her, playing with the change in his trouser pocket. His expression changes, as he brings out a handful of coins.)

I knew it! That ruddy cabby. He's short-changed me. I thought he had, at the time. . . Two bob. What do you make of that, eh? And all on account of that damn garage. They had the car in for servicing only a fortnight ago. . . and now the carburettor goes, You can't rely on anyone. Can't trust a soul. I go to that garage for twenty years, what happens? At the end of the day they let you down. As if you were a complete stranger. If that cab hadn't come. . .

EDITH. Don't get worked up about it, Harry.

(HARRY puts the money back in his pocket.)

HARRY. Sure. . . what's the point? The one thing. . . the only thing. . . that matters. . . that really matters. . . is that we've got you home. . . safe and sound. . .

(EDITH takes his hand. HARRY sits beside her.)

25

HARRY. Look, Edith. . . I'd have been to see you every day . . .

EDITH. I didn't expect you to. There was no need.

HARRY. I should have been. But . . . well, things became so hectic at the office . . . I ended up working late, most nights . . . Heaven knows why. The audit's months away. And my nerves . . . weren't too good . . . nothing to worry about . . . just . . . well, I didn't want to . . . worry you . . .

EDITH. The important thing was your being able to call for me today. The two of you. And thanks again for the flowers, Harry. They're beautiful.

HARRY. Where he finds the money, I don't know.

(Pause.)

Edith . . . I'm so glad they . . . put your mind . . . our minds . . . at rest. The fact that you're . . . in the clear . . .

EDITH. Yes dear . . . in the clear . . .

HARRY. I can't believe it, Edith . . . I still can't take it in . . .

EDITH. It's a weight off our minds, isn't it.

HARRY. To have it spelled out . . . it's wonderful . . . so it is. . . I was sure they'd give you the all clear. . . I couldn't stomach the thought of you . . . having to bear something . . . you didn't deserve . . .

EDITH. We can't always count on getting what we deserve out of life, can we? One way, or the other.

HARRY. The thought of you . . . suffering . . . being made to suffer . . . in any way . . . *(Pause)*. It must have been strange, for you . . . being nursed, instead of doing the nursing . . . They really treated you all right, did they?

EDITH. They couldn't have been kinder.

(Pause)

Or . . . more reassuring . . .

(HARRY *says nothing.* EDITH *glances at him. She sees some folders.*)

What are these?

HARRY. They're Tom's.

EDITH. For his Market Research?

HARRY. He doesn't do Market Research. All he does is the donkey-work. Going round the doors, asking inane questions. Filling in forms.

EDITH. What happens then?

HARRY. Who cares? He's frittering away his time.

EDITH. He's still young, Harry.

HARRY. He's been in Easy Street, all his life. School, university . . .

(EDITH *rises.*)

EDITH. Harry, there's something I've got to ask you.

(As he looks up:) Something . . . I'd like your permission for.

HARRY. You know you can do whatever you want, with or without my permission.

(She sits, centre.)

EDITH. Not this. From a legal viewpoint. I need your approval, as next of kin.

(HARRY *looks at her, sits opposite her.*)

While I was in hospital, they were so good to me . . . so considerate . . . that I decided . . . when I died . . . I've given the matter a lot of thought, Harry . . . I wouldn't dream of mentioning it, otherwise . . . I've decided I'd like . . . to leave my body. So that it might be of use, for research purposes . . . To the Infirmary. Does that appal you?

(Pause. HARRY rises, moves away.)

HARRY. I must admit it's a bit of a . . . bolt from the blue.

EDITH. If you'd prefer to think about it.

27

HARRY. It's your decision, Edith. I wouldn't dream
of . . . standing in your way . . .

EDITH. It doesn't . . . offend you?

HARRY. So long as you don't expect me to follow suit.

EDITH. Thanks, Harry. I'm grateful. Everyone was so
helpful . . . And I felt . . . I feel I want to do . . .
whatever little I can, in return.

HARRY. That's it settled then. No need to raise the
subject again.

EDITH. There'll be the form to sign. And I'll have to
ask Tom.

HARRY. Is that necessary?

EDITH. He's entitled to know, Harry . . . Think how
he'd feel, if he were to find out later.

HARRY. Not that he'll give a tinker's, one way or the
other. Water off a duck's back. You'll see.

(The doorbell rings.)

Guess who!

EDITH. Be nice to her, Harry.

HARRY. She'll have been sitting down there with her
ear to the door all morning. You'll soon be
wishing you were back in hospital. For peace and
quiet.

EDITH. Don't say anything that . . .

*(But he has gone. She rises, glances at her
reflection in the mirror, tidies a stray strand of
hair.)*

HARRY. *(Off)* Hello, Mrs Tait! Nice to see you!

(ELLA *enters, followed by* HARRY. *She carries a
pot of honey.)*

ELLA. She's through here, is she? . . . I was just saying
to Mr. R. here, what a joy to see you back. *(To
HARRY)* It must have been such a worry. *(To
EDITH)* I'm so glad everything's turned out for
the best. I mean it has, hasn't it? I knew it would.
(To HARRY) I'd have come up sooner, but I

28

didn't want to intrude . . . I wanted to give you
time to . . . *(Turns to* EDITH*)* well, to get settled,
you know . . . *(She sees the flowers)* My, what
lovely flowers . . . It's a like the Botanics, so it is.
They'll be from the menfolk, is that right? I
thought so . . . That's just a wee pot of honey for
you, Edith . . . It's clover, not heather. But I hope
you like it, all the same.

EDITH.   I'm sure I will. It's good of you.

ELLA.   I know she has a sweet tooth . . . is that not
right?

EDITH.   And you've been far too kind, while I was
away, Ella . . . Bringing up soup . . . Harry was
telling me . . .

ELLA.   Couldn't have him fading away, could we? You
know what men are like, on their own . . . See
Frank? Opening a tin of beans is about his limit.
That and salami. I must admit he's a dab hand at
slicing the salami.

EDITH.   You'll stay for a cup of tea? Harry's put the
kettle on.

ELLA.   A quick one then. I mustn't stay too long.
(She sits)

(HARRY *exits to the kitchen.)*

EDITH.   Tell me, how has Frank been?

ELLA.   Not so good, this past couple of weeks. It's
partly the papers, I think. They depress him. And
what's going on round about. It seems to get him
down. It's change all the time, so it is. Even the
old bandstand's away. Frank used to spend hours
up there, sitting in the sun. What sun there was.

EDITH.   At least he still has the Gardens.

ELLA.   And the Kibble Palace. He can spend hours in
there . . . watching the goldfish. As if he was . . .
mesmerised.

EDITH.   Does he manage out much?

ELLA.   Hardly at all. He has to watch. He used to follow
the Thistle. But he hasn't been, for donkeys. It's

29

too much for him. Pedestrians, even. The last time
he cut up past the Pewter Pot, he said two Red
Indians tried to assassinate him.

(HARRY *comes in with a tea tray, and puts it
down.*)

HARRY.   Maybe he meant West Indians.

EDITH.   You must be worried sick, Ella . . .

HARRY.   Unless they were Hearts supporters.

EDITH.   . . . being cooped up all day, like that.

ELLA.   All his landmarks are changing . . .

EDITH.   Are there any biscuits, Harry?

HARRY.   I'll look, in the tin. *(He exits to the kitchen.)*

ELLA.   What was it like in hospital, Edith? Not too bad?

EDITH.   They couldn't have been kinder.

ELLA.   Of course they've got all those modern appliances
now. Not like in your day. Still, you can never
tell . . .

EDITH.   What do you mean?

ELLA.   Well, funny things can happen . . . Take Beryl's
cousin Olive . . . it's her half-cousin, really . . .
the one with the birthmark . . . she came out with
half her stomach missing. Blamed the language
barrier. Not that Olive's too bright, mind you. She
was the one, when her first was due, and she didn't
want her man to know, she made up her mind to
keep it a secret from him. And we said, how on
earth could she do that? And she said, I'll tell him
it's my periods piling up!

(HARRY *comes in with the teapot, and biscuits on
a plate. He puts them down.*)

(To EDITH) Men can't take it, can they? The
majority. Anything to do with B & W makes them
squeamish.

HARRY.   What's B & W?

EDITH.   Bowels and Wombs.

HARRY.   I'm sure Edith doesn't want to talk about that
that . . . now she's home.

ELLA.   See what I mean, Edith!

(Tea is poured. HARRY *does not have any.)*

Have you a minute, Mr. R? There was something
I wanted to ask you. Do you get the knocking . . .
up here?

HARRY.   What knocking?

ELLA.   Maybe not a knocking . . . so much as . . . a dull
thudding . . . a sort of vibrating . . . Frank calls
them his vibrations . . . he says he doesn't so much
hear them . . . as feel them . . .

EDITH.   Downstairs, you mean?

ELLA.   For a while I thought they were in his head . . .
you know . . . but now I'm not so sure. The last
couple of evenings, I've heard them too . . .

(EDITH *and* HARRY *looks at each other.)*

I know what you're thinking . . . but I wondered . . .
The basement through the wall from us has newly
opened as a judo and krate club *(She mispronoun-
ces the word)*

(HARRY flinches.)

I thought maybe these noises . . . might be people . . .
landing on the mat . . . or whatever . . .

HARRY.   *(Corrects her)* K*a*rate.

EDITH.   How does Frank react?

ELLA.   That's the worry. He thinks it's the Chinese
coming to get him. He sits up in a cold sweat, so
he does . . . listening.   The other evening, he told
me to bolt the door. What for, I said. Against Mao
Tse-Chung, he replied. And his equestrian hordes!
It's getting worse than the time he thought the
Russians were spying on him, through the tellie.
You know Edith, it's awful . . . Sometimes he has
me near believing him.

HARRY.   He isn't too hot at the politics.

ELLA.   You can say that again. He keeps giving me
letters to post to Winston Churchill.

EDITH.   The judo club must have opened while I was
away. I thought it wasn't till next month?

31

HARRY.   Plenty of cars roll up.

EDITH.   What astonishes me, is that they can open a judo club in a residential area.

HARRY.   No such thing as a residential area nowadays. Same as so-called green belt. Only there, to be eaten into. We're the ones to suffer, time and time again. The pigs in the middle. No one to protect our interests. Guard our privacy.

ELLA.   You think it must be the club then?

HARRY.   If it is, we'll put a stop to it. We can nab them on any number of grounds. For parking. Or creating a disturbance. They'll be wanting a licence next, you'll see.

EDITH.   But what can we do, Harry? In practical terms?

HARRY.   Organise a petition. A round robin.

EDITH.   The trouble is, people won't raise a finger unless their own privileges are threatened.

ELLA.   If these vibrations get worse, I don't know what Frank'll do. How it might affect him. Edith, I'm almost at the end of my tether.

HARRY.   *(Crosses from the window)* You're right. Nothing's sacred. Desecration, left, right and centre. They're turning it into a concrete jungle. A desert. All the old property is being swept aside. . . the old values with it . . .

EDITH.   Harry . . .

HARRY.   *(Turns to ELLA)* I'll see what I can do. Drop a word in the right place. The right ear. On the Q.T. I'll get it looked into. If it gets any worse. Don't worry . . .if that's what's the root of the trouble, we'll soon have them . . . by the short and curlies.

ELLA.   I knew I could rely on you. I'm at . . . such a loss, always.

(She finishes her tea, spreads out her hand as EDITH offers her a second cup.)

No thanks, I mustn't overstay my welcome. In any case, I best be getting back down to Frank.

32

EDITH. Are you fixed up, for the summer?

ELLA. Oh yes . . . you have to book so far in advance now, don't you. We're going back to the same place. I was tempted to change. Frank's sister Olive fancied Torremolinos. But Frank couldn't cope. In any case these resorts are dead common, so they are. Ingrid said, last year when they went, her and Andy . . . the first thing they heard over the wall of their hotel was "Hey, hoo's about wee headies on the pashio!"

HARRY. Lucky there was a hotel at all.

ELLA. *(Rises)* Here, Frank'll be thinking I've eloped. I promised to put a flan in the oven for him . . . If there's one thing he loves, it's flan. Oh, tell Tom I've a yoghourt started again. I'll bring one up for him this evening. Thanks, Mr. R . . . It's good to know we can count on you. Don't bother seeing me out, if I don't know my way by now . . .

(But HARRY does follow her out.)

EDITH. *(Calls)* Thanks again for the honey, Ella.

(The front door closes, off. HARRY comes in.)

Pour soul . . .

HARRY. She's a pain in the tonsils. *(He takes the tray and tea things to the hatch.)*

EDITH. Think of the time she's had . . . with Frank. Do you think it is the karate club that's doing it?

HARRY. I don't see how we can help.

EDITH. His view of things . . . his perspectives . . . must be distorted . . . so different from ours . . . Sounds, too . . . I can understand him being disturbed . . . Believing they were coming for him . . . *(She shivers slightly)* We are fortunate, Harry . . . in relation to some people . . .

(HARRY *approaches her.)*

HARRY. Edith . . .

(It looks as though he is on the point of kissing her, when:

33

TOM *enters, sees them standing there.)*

TOM.   Happy families!

EDITH.   Hello, dear.

TOM.   Sudden embarrassment, as junior member of tribe intrudes on intimate scene, removes sweaty over-garment, rubs clammy hands, and sits in recently vacated chair still oozing warmth from denizon of basement flat.

(TOM *sits where* ELLA *had been.)*

Nosh finished?

EDITH.   Did you see Ella?

TOM.   Almost bumped into her, on the stair. Five seconds sooner, I'd have had my onions. As it was I stood, breath bated, doing my noted impersonation of a hatstand. By which time she had shuffled back to Zombie-ville.

EDITH.   Tom!

HARRY.   The boy's right. There's no point in hiding it.

EDITH.   I think it's a terrible thing to say.

TOM.   Facing facts. He sits all day, at the window, staring into thin air . . . doesn't see a thing . . . Like a stookie . . . a tailor's dummie . . . Gives me the creeps, so he does. *(He takes the car keys from his pocket; throws them to* HARRY) Damp plugs.

(EDITH *goes towards the kitchen.)*

HARRY.   Where are you going, Edith?

EDITH.   I'll do the tea dishes. It won't take a minute.

HARRY.   You'll nothing of the kind. *(Pause)* Tom can do them.

TOM.   Thanks a lot! I've the table to set. I'll do all the dishes afterwards, at the same time. Save hot water. *(He makes an exaggerated grin, at* HARRY *who does not respond.)*

Was she telling you about Frank's vibrations?

EDITH.   She was asking your father's advice. *(To* HARRY) You shouldn't encourage her to think

34

you are in a position to help, Harry.

TOM.   Doing his big Ombudsman bit again, was he?

HARRY.   I was simply trying to put her mind at rest.

TOM.   You've a hope.

EDITH.   Is lunch taken care of?

HARRY.   Tom was getting everything.

TOM.   Tom has got everything. Surprise, surprise!
(To EDITH*)* It's only cold meat salad. We can have
it in the kitchen.

EDITH.   Can I give you a hand?

HARRY.   *(Sharply)* Edith, will you sit down and let us
get on with it.

TOM.   Don't speak to her, like that.

HARRY.   Your mother's newly out of hospital.

TOM.   That's all the more reason.

HARRY.   All I'm doing is telling her to sit down. While
you and I get on with . . . whatever has to be done.

TOM.   Surely *she* knows whether she wants to sit down
or not.

EDITH.   Tom, hang your coat in the hall, dear.

(As he goes.) And could you bring my cardigan?

(TOM *exits.* HARRY *lifts the ties.)*

HARRY.   These, when you're at it . . . *(he slings them
over a chair, leans on it.)*

EDITH.   I'll be fine, Harry.

HARRY.   You mustn't . . . over-exhaust yourself . . .

(TOM *comes in, sees* HARRY, *makes a matador
pass at him with the cardigan:* HARRY *grabs it.*
TOM *grins, exits to the kitchen.)*

Would you like the heater on? Are you sure? I
hope you haven't caught a chill . . .

(Sounds of TOM *setting the table, off. Cutlery.*
EDITH*'s arm sticks, in the cardigan sleeve:*

HARRY *helps her on with it.)*

TOM. *(At the hatch)* The age of chivalry is not yet dead! I'll need spoons. I got some ice-cream.

HARRY. In this weather!

EDITH. That'll be lovely, dear.

(She crosses to the sideboard, opens a drawer, takes out the spoons and lays them on the hatch.)

HARRY. By the way, where's my sports jacket?

TOM. *(Off)* Thanks for reminding me.

HARRY. Don't say you forgot.

EDITH. Even if the boy has forgotten, Harry . . . you aren't likely to need it over the weekend.

(TOM *comes in.)*

TOM. Don't you believe it. He's taking up golf again.

HARRY. Well, have you?

TOM. Nope.

EDITH. It'll be in your wardrobe.

TOM. Nope.

HARRY. Did you forget it?

TOM. Nope.

HARRY. Where is it, then?

TOM. I didn't forget the jacket, I forgot the ticket.

HARRY. Clown!

TOM. Or someone forgot to give me it. I don't like being called that.

HARRY. You'll have to learn to put up with a lot of things you don't like in life.

EDITH. Put on a pullover, if you're cold.

HARRY. I'm not cold.

TOM. Then what do you want your jacket for?

(HARRY *turns on his heels and leaves the room.)*

36

EDITH. *(Calls)* If you care to wash your hands, Harry . . .
You too, Tom. You mustn't rile your father like
that.

TOM. Him that riles me. *(Then, loudly enough for
HARRY to hear)* I'll collect his jacket this
afternoon. *(Pause)* If he asks me nicely.

EDITH. I'm asking you, dear.

TOM. Beneath his dignity, is it? *(He goes to the kitchen)*

EDITH. Ella said she'd bring up some yoghourt, this
evening.

TOM. *(Off)* Not on the carpet, I hope.

(TOM *has placed a bottle, wrapped in brown
paper, on the hatch. He comes in, takes three
glasses from the sideboard, picks up the bottle
and unwraps it.*)

EDITH. Tom . . .

TOM. A tiny gesture . . . to celebrate your return . . .
After all, it's a red-letter day. *(He puts the bottle
down: Sherry)*

(EDITH *rises.*)

EDITH. Does your father know?

TOM. He didn't pay for it, if that's what you mean.
Anyway, why worry? He doesn't need to have
any, if he doesn't want to. Remember we always
used to . . . have a sherry . . . on Saturdays . . . ?
(He pours three sherries)

(HARRY *enters, a pullover over his head. He
draws it on. As he sees the bottle, he stops dead.
He looks at* TOM, *then at* EDITH, *but says
nothing.* TOM *corks the bottle. He lifts two
glasses, hands one to* EDITH *and offers one to*
HARRY.

HARRY *does not take it.* TOM *puts the glass
down, returns to the sideboard for his own,
raises it.*)

Cheers anyway . . . Happy families!

HARRY. What do you think you're doing?

37

TOM. You'll swelter in that.

EDITH. You needn't take it, Harry . . . It was . . . for my coming home, that's all . . . a gesture.

HARRY. *(Directed at* TOM) Some bloody gesture.

TOM. *(Quietly)* Of course, I forgot . . . this is a dry area . . . The terrace, I mean . . . Why didn't you remind me? It must be years since a drop of alcohol passed these portals . . .

EDITH. There's no reason for your father to have a sherry, if he doesn't want to. In any case maybe he'd prefer it . . . after he's carved the meat . . .

TOM. I'll manage. *(Glass in hand, he exits to the kitchen)*

EDITH. Please, Harry . . . for my sake . . . *(And in a slightly different tone)* I'm not . . . really fond of . . . formal toasts . . . I think we should just . . . sip our sherry . . .

(There comes the sound of a carving-knife being whetted: rhythmic, steel upon steel. EDITH exits to the kitchen.

HARRY lifts his glass, holds it as though about to crush it, then pours the sherry carefully back into the bottle. With a glance at the hatch he crosses to the bookcase, brings out the whisky bottle, fills his glass, replaces the bottle behind the row of books.

HARRY glances in the mirror, dabs his chin. He heads for the kitchen.)

END OF ACT ONE

ACT TWO

Scene 1

Late afternoon.

The sherry bottle is gone. The flowers are on the sideboard.

HARRY *is at the table. He has a ledger-sized loose-leaf book, upholstery samples, a pot of glue and brush, and a metal tray. He is gumming the pattern-samples, and putting them in the book with a care and concentration out of proportion to the difficulty of the task. He takes a blotting-pad, presses it on the page he has been working on.*

EDITH *sits, starts to sew.*

EDITH.   How many's that now?

HARRY.   No idea. Haven't counted. But I'm onto the plain ones, so I must be at least half-way. *(He continues)* That's one more. Straight as a die.

(Snip of EDITH's *scissors.)*

EDITH.   You're missing the Sport. Did the tellie men not come?

HARRY.   I'm as good getting on with this.

EDITH.   Did you manage to cope with the milk-boy?

HARRY.   I left Tom to handle that.

EDITH. . I must leave a note for them on Monday. We can start another pint again. *(Pause)* Harry, how were things . . . while I was away?

HARRY.   There's something the matter with this glue.

EDITH.   You don't need to . . . hide anything, from me . . .

HARRY.   I've been . . . fit as a fiddle . . . if it wasn't for my nerves. If it wasn't for that . . . everything'd be hunkey-dorey.

EDITH.   And the office?

HARRY.   This glue's gone off. *(And he sniffs it)*

39

EDITH.   Has everything settled down?

HARRY.   Everything's . . . synthetic, these days. Nothing made of . . . natural substances, any more . . . Yes it has. In any case I had McCallum taped. And he knew it. My God, all he was wanting was for me to make way for a younger man. Wanted me to "groom" him. For my own job! I told him, any more of his tricks, I'd cook his goose for him. Because his name's on the notepaper doesn't entitle him to treat me like dirt. If he tries that again. . .

EDITH.   You'll be careful, Harry. You can't afford to antagonise him.

HARRY.   I can't afford to lose my self-respect.

EDITH.   I realise that, Harry.

HARRY.   Public school smarm, that's all McCallum is. Him and his type. Daddy's money and a big Jag, they think they're . . . Mind you . . . *(As he concentrates on what he is doing)* Mind you . . . I'm maybe not . . . as fast, as I used to be . . . I can get the job done, but it sometimes takes . . . well, a little longer . . . stands to reason, doesn't it . . . Can't teach an old dog . . .

(She makes no response, but continues sewing: then suddenly:)

What did you mean, hide anything from you?

EDITH.   We needn't have any secrets. From one another. You don't have to do anything behind my back . . . for fear of hurting me. When does McCallum go South, anyway?

HARRY.   Bugger McCallum! (HARRY *rises, crosses to the bookcase, brings out his bottle, goes to the sideboard, pours a whisky.)* Know what I could do with? *(Pause)* A refreshment. *(Pause)* How about you? No? Mind if I . . . help myself? Thirsty work this . . .

Well, down the river! *(He drinks)* Sure you wouldn't fancy something? Ginger beer?

EDITH.   No thanks, dear.

HARRY.   Where's Tom going tonight?

EDITH.   The Cosmo I think.

HARRY.   I thought he might have stayed in, on your first night home.

EDITH.   Maybe he will. Not that there's any need to.

HARRY.   He's getting nowhere fast.

EDITH.   Give the boy time, dear.

HARRY.   Not time he needs, it's initiative.

EDITH.   Isn't he waiting to hear from the television people?

HARRY.   He's heard.

EDITH.   Did they turn him down?

HARRY.   He turned them down.

EDITH.   Wasn't it good enough for him?

HARRY.   Damn sight too good. He doesn't know which side his bread's buttered. He'll be a dustman for a couple of months, because they're the salt of the earth. But anything more permanent, anything commensurate with his ability, he turns up his nose at it.

EDITH.   At least he has his degree up his sleeve.

HARRY.   It'd do as much good up his backside. You talk about his degree, as if it were some sort of . . . talisman. Degrees are ten a penny. It's what you do with them that counts. He's throwing his down the drain. He has nothing to show for himself. He's a waster. A wishbone for a backbone. Think of it, a son of mine . . . *(He drinks)*

EDITH.   That's what riles you, isn't it?

HARRY.   For crying out loud, he doesn't even go in for sport. Never put a toe in the water, that I can remember. Says he abhors the competitive element.

EDITH.   Maybe he has something. There's been far too much competition . . . phoney competitiveness . . . forced on children Tom's age.

HARRY.   He isn't a child now. That's what you keep forgetting.

41

EDITH. When he was a child. All through school. Prizes for this, prizes for that. Then the Bursary Comp. Instead of each pupil, each student, being of value for himself. It was each one against his neighbour. Thank heaven, young people today seem to resist it. The rat race we've imposed on them. They simply opt out.

HARRY. Look at them! You can smell them a mile away . . .

EDITH. You're generalising.

HARRY. You're romanticising.

EDITH. In any case, Tom doesn't seem to feel obliged to identify with them . . . any more than with us. That's one thing I admire him for. He's level-headed, Harry. He's never been one for extremes.

(HARRY *has finished his drink.*)

HARRY. Extremes of idleness.

EDITH. Harry . . . every father wants to express himself . . . to fulfil himself, through his son. Nothing wrong with that. But Tom has a personality of his own. You can't hold sway over him, Harry. Not any longer. You must let him . . . lead his own life . . .

(HARRY *pours another drink.*)

HARRY. If I thought he would fulfil himself . . . I want him to succeed. To make something of himself. In the world.

EDITH. To make up for you? To compensate?

HARRY. I wasn't born with a silver spoon in my mouth. But at his age, I'd made a start. I had my foot on the ladder. Even if it was the bottom rung. I know I didn't make the top. And I'm damned glad I didn't. But I'd made a start. It's cut-throat at the top. Accountancy, advertising, anywhere you like. I cut my cloth. I refused to kow-tow, when the secretaryships were being doled out. My face didn't fit. So they squeezed me out.

EDITH. So you want Tom to get up the ladder you never got up.

HARRY. At least I want him to *succeed*. You sound as if you'd prefer him to *fail*.

EDITH. Why would I want that?

HARRY. Because your own career was interrupted. By the state of . . . holy matrimony . . . being inflicted on you.

EDITH. You know perfectly well I was only nursing because of the War.

HARRY. I mean teaching. You never got back to teacher training college.

EDITH. I was never cut out to be a teacher.

HARRY. None the less, you're still trying . . . because of that . . . to take it out on the boy.

EDITH. On Tom!

HARRY. On Tom, on me. I mean, there was a time I was promising . . . and see how I've ended up. Tom isn't even promising!

EDITH. He's full of ideas.

HARRY. They never come to anything. They're like. . . flies buzzing about inside a Toshie lantern.

EDITH. Perhaps we haven't given him enough encouragement.

HARRY. Who's fed and clothed him? Seen him through university? Who's still subsidising him?

EDITH. Enough stimulus, then? I mean . . . were we always there, when he needed us?

HARRY. I was there. The trouble was, I could never get near him. For you. You mollycoddled him, made a mummy's boy of him.

EDITH. You washed your hands of him.

HARRY. You turned him against me.

EDITH. You opted out. From the start.

HARRY. I'm his father, and entitled to his respect. It's high time he recognised that.

EDITH. You cannot command respect. You have to earn it.

HARRY.   As his father. And mark my words, I'll have
it. If I have to whip it out of him.

EDITH.   You'll only make a laughing-stock of yourself.

(He drinks.)

HARRY.   You think I haven't noticed? The two of
you? Sniggering behind my back, every chance
you get? That business of the sherry . . . you used
that . . . The two of you ganging up . . .

EDITH.   You're sidestepping the issue.

HARRY.   I'm getting to the heart of it.

EDITH.   You're setting up a smokescreen.

HARRY.   Always the same. You egg me on, make out
you approve of what I do, then turn your back
and withdraw your sanction . . . so that you can
store it, harbour it, against me. *(He drinks, crosses
the room)* He's careful, I grant you. He goads me.
But he always manages to stop, short of the limit.
But one of these days he'll over-step the mark.
He'll sail too close to the wind. And by God I'll
have him, if it's the last thing I do.

EDITH.   You say that . . . with such relish . . .

(Pause.)

HARRY.   He has no values.

EDITH.   That's not true. He may have examined ours,
and found them wanting. That doesn't entitle you
to dismiss his.

HARRY.   You're blaming me, again?

EDITH.   If anyone's to blame, we both are. We're
equally responsible for him.

HARRY.   Responsible?

EDITH.   Morally responsible.

*(He finishes his drink, pours another. A pause,
before:)*

All I mean is . . . we're not . . . we can't hold
ourselves up . . . as paragons. It stands to reason.

HARRY.   In what way are we . . . morally responsible?

EDITH. I'd have thought it was obvious.

HARRY. You mean reprehensible?

EDITH. Don't ask me to spell it out for you.

HARRY. That's what I'd like you to do. Spell it out.

EDITH. All I'm saying is that we can't evade the
consequences . . . the implications . . . of Tom
being born. The . . . the circumstances . . . of his
birth.

(HARRY *swivels round.*)

Look Harry . . . any parents . . . well, they must
face up to . . .

HARRY. You're not talking about any parents. You're
talking about us. About you and me. If I'd
realised that was what . . . That's below the belt,
so it is. You're thinking . . . of us . . . the
"circumstances" of his birth . . .

EDITH. You're twisting what I said.

HARRY. You've harboured that against me . . . all
those years . . . to bring it up now . . . to use as
ammunition . . . against me . . . after all that
time . . .

EDITH. You're imagining things.

HARRY. You'll be telling me next I imagined what
happened, all those years ago. That I imagined
things . . . behind the Pool.

EDITH. For God's sake, Harry . . .

HARRY. Behind the Pool . . . in Bill Smith's little
green van . . . the windows steamed up . . . You
and me . . . in the back seat . . .

EDITH. This is disgusting.

HARRY. You didn't think so, at the time. Or if you
did, you hid it well. Your disgust, I mean. If you
didn't enjoy it, you made a bloody good
pretence . . . *(He drains his glass.)* I don't deserve
my son's respect . . . because there were no white
sheets and bridal suites, when we first made love . . .
Because I sullied . . . young Edith . . . all those
years ago . . .

45

EDITH. Please . . .

HARRY. You talk about morality? Where's your
morality? You only married me, because you
thought you had to.

EDITH. God help me, Harry . . . I married you . . .
because I loved you.

HARRY. If I'd only known . . . you wouldn't have
sunk your claws in so easily . . . If I'd had my wits
about me, I wouldn't have ended up in this bloody
hole . . .

EDITH. Harry . . .

HARRY. You married me . . . as a substitute. Are you
listening? As a substitute . . . for someone else. In
place of the real hero. The one . . . who didn't
come back . . . to collect . . . what he'd won . . .

(The sounds of their breathing, then:)

EDITH. You found out? While I was in hospital?

HARRY. I always suspected. Then the other evening,
when I was looking for the nightdress you wanted
me to bring, in the drawer, I found the box with
the medal, the letters in their ribbon . . .

EDITH. Harry, you're wrong . . . I'm sorry, but you're
wrong . . . I swear you're . . .

HARRY. It's not for you . . . to be sorry. In any case,
being sorry . . . doesn't cancel it out, does it.
(Pause) It must have been some devil that . . . got
into me . . . *(He rises slowly, moves towards the
sideboard)*

EDITH. Harry!

(He stops in his tracks, but does not look at her.)

Give me your shirt. I'll sew that button on, while
I'm at it.

HARRY. How can you . . .?

EDITH. It won't take a minute.

*(He takes off his pullover, then the shirt. She holds
out an arm. He drapes the shirt over it.*

Thanks. *(She prepares to sew the button on)*

46

(Pause.)

HARRY. *(To himself)* And . . . the citation . . .

EDITH. Mmm?

HARRY. What's the bloody use . . .?

(Pause.

The front door slams, off.

They freeze, for a moment. Then HARRY *heads for the sideboard.)*

Always slamming doors . . .

(HARRY *takes the bottle and glass, exits to the kitchen.*

TOM *comes in from the hall. He has* HARRY's *jacket on a hanger. He throws a pink evening paper on the table and lays the jacket on the back of a chair.)*

TOM. Better not let Frank see the results, or he'll have a relapse. *(He takes off his coat, throws it on the sofa.)*

HARRY. *(Off)* How did the Accies get on?

TOM. I haven't read the small print.

(HARRY *enters from the kitchen.* TOM *does a double-take, at the sight of him in his singlet. As* HARRY *is about to put on his pullover:)*

Been doing your Mick McManus bit again? How about a touch of the old Boston crabs?

(TOM *confronts* HARRY, *shoulders hunched, hands jiggling under his armpits.)*

Ho-ho!

(It looks as though HARRY *will not respond. But he does, taking up a similar stance facing* TOM.)*

HARRY. Grrr . . .

TOM. Grrrrr . . .

HARRY. Grrrrr . . .

TOM. Grrrrrrrrrr!!!

(They grapple. TOM twists HARRY's arm behind his back.)

HARRY.   What the blazes . . .

TOM.   Sorry, it was an accident.

EDITH.   Stop it, you two.

HARRY.   One of these days . . .

EDITH.   Tom has collected your sports jacket, Harry.

HARRY.   I hope they've done a decent job of it.

(TOM sniffs, makes a drinking gesture behind HARRY's back.)

EDITH.   Tom, have you bought any new tricks, since I went away?

TOM.   You call them effects. Or illusions. Not tricks. *(Pause)* Yes, I got one I've had my eye on for some time. It's the kind . . .

EDITH.   Why don't you show it to us? It's an ideal opportunity, isn't it Harry, when the television's broken? Harry?

HARRY.   Sure . . . sure . . .

TOM.   I love it when Dad bubbles with enthusiasm!

EDITH.   Please, Tom . . . we'd love to see it . . .

HARRY.   I hope it's not those billiard balls again . . . Can I clear the table for you?

TOM.   You know I've got my own table.

HARRY.   Sorry . . .

(TOM exits.)

EDITH.   At least he's enthusiastic about it, Harry . . . It won't take long.

(EDITH finishes sewing on the button. She holds out his shirt. HARRY puts it on.)

HARRY.   Thanks.

(EDITH puts her sewing things in the box, puts the box by the window. HARRY positions her chair, and his own. TOM enters, with his conjuring table:

48

it has a silver tripod and black cover.)

EDITH.   Who was the most famous magician, Tom?

HARRY.   Houdini. Harry Houdini. Wasn't he?

TOM.   He was more of an escapologist. Levant, maybe.
He made elephants appear on stage.

HARRY.   He must have had a big hat.

TOM.   Or Chung Ling-Su.

HARRY.   Sounds like a pal of Frank's.

TOM.   He was an American. Used to catch a bullet in
his teeth.

HARRY.   All done by mirrors, I bet.

TOM.   Till it went wrong, and he was shot through the
heart.

(TOM *has switched on and positioned the standard
lamp. He returns to his table. He lays* HARRY's
*jacket on the sofa, and returns to the table. On the
conjuring table: a pack of cards; a hollow chrome
cylinder, with two circles of tissue and two metal
clips; a magic wand, black with white tips; a silk
top-hat; and a bottle round which is wound a
length of white rope.*

TOM *picks up the cards, takes them from their
packet.)*

TOM.   Here we have . . . an ordinary deck of cards . . .

HARRY.   That's a lie, for a start. Or he wouldn't bother
telling us.

TOM.   . . . which I shuffle . . . so . . .

HARRY.   *(Sotto)* They're all marked.

TOM.   You may examine them if you wish, Sir . . .

EDITH.   They're my whist cards, Harry . . .

(TOM *fans the cards in front of* HARRY, *face
down,* HARRY *puts on his spectacles.)*

TOM.   Would you please take one, Sir . . . Any one you
like . . .

HARRY.   Hold them steady . . .

49

(TOM *does so.*)

TOM. Make sure you've a free choice . . . that I'm not forcing one on you . . .

(HARRY *picks a card.*)

HARRY. Now what do you want me to do?

TOM. If you'd look at it, and show it to the lady . . . without letting me see it . . .

(As HARRY *does so:)*

. . . and replace it . . . on top of the deck.

(HARRY *shows* EDITH *the card, allowing the audience to see it at the same time: then puts it on the pack.*)

HARRY. On top. I knew there'd be a catch.

TOM. And cut . . . (TOM *cuts the pack cleanly*) Now, shuffle the cards . . . *(He shuffles them)* And . . .

HARRY. How about letting me shuffle them?

TOM. Certainly, Sir.

(*To* HARRY's *surprise,* TOM *lets him do so.* TOM *takes the cards.*)

Now Sir, would you mind telling me what your card was?

HARRY. Not on your nellie.

TOM. Please? What was your card?

HARRY. You tell me!

EDITH. Come on, Harry.

HARRY. What's the point of the trick, if . . . *(Grudgingly)* Jack of Diamonds.

(TOM *hands the cards to* EDITH.)

TOM. Would you see if you can find the Jack of Diamonds, Madam.

(EDITH *looks through the cards.*)

EDITH. It doesn't seem to be there.

HARRY. Of course it's there. I've just put it in.

(HARRY *takes the cards, looks through them himself. He looks baffled.*)

TOM.   What did you say your card was again, Sir . . . the Jack of Diamonds? Is that your sports jacket? I wonder, would you mind looking in the top pocket . . . if you would . . . thank you . . .

(HARRY *does so, brings out a card.*)

And would you tell us what the card is?

(HARRY *holds the card up.*)

HARRY.   Jack of Diamonds!

(TOM *bows to* HARRY, *receives the card from him, lays it down.*

EDITH *claps.*)

TOM.   Thank you very much, Sir. *(And he gestures for* HARRY *to sit)*

EDITH.   Very good, Tom . . . You must admit, Harry . . .

TOM.   Now . . . *(He picks up the chrome cylinder and the wand)* This is what is called a ghost tube. For obvious reasons. Because . . . *(As he passes the wand through it, and holds it out for* EDITH *and* HARRY — *and the audience* — *to look through)* it is absolutely empty . . . as you can see for yourselves . . . Now in ancient China, magicians could take empty tubes, just like this . . . and fasten a piece of tissue over each end . . . like so . . . *(He does so, and puts the metal clip on top)* so that . . . we end up with a hollow tube . . . enclosed at both ends . . . *(He holds it up)* But once again, if I take the magic wand . . . and give the tube two taps, one hot, one cold . . . *(He taps it.)* Abracadabra . . . we can open the tube . . . " and find . . .

(He bursts the tissue at one end, puts his fingers neatly inside the tube, and brings out a red chiffon square. Then a yellow, then a green—then a whole stream of silks.

EDITH *applauds again.*)

HARRY.   Very good . . . they didn't come down his sleeve . . . I was on the look-out for that . . . Yes, very colourful . . .

(TOM *has put down the tube and the coloured silks.*)

Let's see it again!

TOM.   Not on your life. That's the golden rule. Or someone'll see through the effect.

EDITH.   Why do you suppose your father asked!

(TOM *takes the bottle and the rope. He steps away from his table, and chats relaxedly, apparently not as part of his conjuring routine but in an explanatory way:*)

TOM.   Some effects are relatively easy . . . like that one with the ghost tube . . . or like the one with the cards, where it was the gentleman himself who actually performed it for me . . . Others can be more complex. Because they depend on some piece of machinery, or a subtle bit of misdirection on the part of the magician. Others rely on clever patter, for their impact. But there are a few . . . only a few . . . which are not tricks, or illusions even . . . so much as sheer magic. Because they are in the cold light of day, to all intents and purposes, quite inexplicable. In others words, impossible. Abra-cadabra!

(He has been allowing the end of the rope to slide up and down inside the neck of the bottle. Now he takes away his supporting hand. The bottle hangs in mid-air, suspended on the rope.)

EDITH.   Tom!

(TOM *bows to* EDITH *and to* HARRY. HARRY *peers at the bottle.* TOM *lets him hold it, and draws the rope out.*)

How do you explain that one, Harry?

TOM.   He couldn't, in a month of Sundays.

(HARRY *puts the bottle on* TOM's *table.*)

HARRY.   Abra-ca-bloody-dabra!

EDITH.   What intrigues me, Tom is the way you . . .

HARRY.   What intrigues me is how much it must have cost.

EDITH. I'm sure it wasn't extortionate.

TOM. Remember you have to pay for the secret as well.

HARRY. Depends what you mean by extortionate.

TOM. It was well within my means, don't worry.

HARRY. You haven't got any means.

EDITH. It's only one trick after all, Harry. . .

HARRY. One trick! His room's heaped with junk.
Almost to the ceiling. Don't tell me he got these for
free. All those catalogues . . . that come by post. . .

TOM. I can always resell it, if I have to.

HARRY. There he goes. . . talking about reselling it. . .
no stickability.

TOM. You needn't worry. There are more important
things in my life than conjuring.

HARRY. Such as?

TOM. Brian's making a film.

HARRY. I hope it's none of your. . . underground muck.

TOM. Don't worry.

EDITH. What are you going to this evening, Tom?

TOM. A Czech film. Doubt if it'll be much good.

HARRY. Why go?

TOM. Buster Keaton's on with it, in "The General".

EDITH. That's more your father's cup of tea.

TOM. They've got talkies now, you know.

HARRY. You'll be going with Brian?

TOM. That's right.

> (HARRY *sighs audibly.*)

> What's up with him?

> *(Pause.)*

HARRY. Before you go. . . There's something your
mother wants to ask you. . . You may as well
ask him now, and get it off your mind, Edith. . .

EDITH. I don't feel now's the time, Harry. . . I'd
rather. . .

TOM. What's all the mystery?

EDITH. There's no mystery.

TOM. Has he been saying something to upset you?

EDITH. No, dear. . . It's simply that. . . when I die. . .

TOM. What!

EDITH. In the fullness of time, Tom. . . I decided I'd
like, when the time comes. . . to. . . This is a
step I wouldn't dream of taking, without your
permission. . . I'd like, with your agreement and
your father's. . . to leave my body, for research.
That's all.

TOM. *(To* HARRY) You knew about this?

(HARRY *nods.)*

(To EDITH) What did he say? He didn't give
you permission?

HARRY. I agreed. Any objections?

EDITH. You don't have to make your mind up
straight away, Tom.

TOM. I don't need to make my mind up at all. I
find it abhorrent. Christ, have you no feelings? At
the idea of her being. . . chopped up, in front of
a shower of students?

HARRY. She won't have any feelings by then, will
she? In any case it's not the University, it's the
Infirmary.

TOM. Why, do the Infirmary pay more? Say I was to
go into a pub, one lunchtime. . . or the Union. . .
and have this medic come up to me and say,
"Hello old boy, I saw your mater this morning".
And I say "I'm afraid you've boobed, old bean, she
died six months ago". And he says, "That's right,
we were slicing her up". Christ, that'd put you off
your steak and kidney.

HARRY. Control yourself.

TOM. I was asked for an opinion.

HARRY. You've given it.

TOM. Isn't there enough going on as it is? Another
heart-transplant in the offing. There was a thing

54

in yesterday's paper. . . about Barnard. . . doing
a blood-swap between a baboon and a woman. . .

HARRY.   What's that got to do with. . .?

TOM.   It's an affront. To human dignity.

HARRY.   It's research.

TOM.   Everything's research. Like all those millions, to
put a man on the moon. All right. Go ahead. Do
what you want. I don't care.

HARRY.   No need to get hysterical.

EDITH.   No one'll do anything against your wishes, Tom.

HARRY.   You're not letting this emotional outburst
affect your decision, are you? All he does is open
his mouth and let his belly rumble.

TOM.   What do you suppose you do? With your great
gob. Swimming round your cosy, self-contained
wee goldfish bowl. . . Well, one of these days,
someone's going to put a brick throught it.

HARRY.   Are you threatening me?

TOM.   Take it any way you like.

HARRY.   Grow up.

EDITH.   I'm sorry I raised the subject, in the first place.

TOM.   He made you.

EDITH.   And I'm sorry I've upset you. I never expected
you to react like this. At the same time that's no
excuse for speaking to your father that way. I'd
like you to apologise.

TOM.   What!

EDITH.   I think you're due your father an apology,
for that outburst. It was quite unjustified.

TOM.   He'll be lucky.

EDITH.   I'm waiting.

(Pause.)

TOM.   I'm sorry. For your sake.

EDITH.   Thank you. I think I'll lie down for a little
while, I feel a bit sleepy. . .

HARRY.   I'm not surprised. . .

TOM.   Look, Mum. . .

EDITH.   *(Sharply)* That's the matter closed. I don't want to refer to it again.

(EDITH *exits.*

HARRY *exits to the kitchen.)*

TOM.   *(Calls)* Topping-up time, is it?

HARRY.   *(Off)* Topping what up?

TOM.   The kettle, of course.

(TOM *picks up the evening paper, starts reading.* HARRY *enters.)*

HARRY.   You're treading on thin ice.

(No reply.)

Your mother asked you, out of courtesy. Not because she had to.

TOM.   Meaning?

HARRY.   Meaning she can go ahead without your permission.

TOM.   She only needs yours?

HARRY.   That's right.

TOM.   So?

HARRY.   You've upset her, needlessly.

TOM.   *I've* upset her!

HARRY.   Why do you always have to go and make a fool of yourself?

TOM.   Maybe it's heredity.

HARRY.   You always act as though you were the only person who counted.

TOM.   You mean I don't count?

HARRY.   I didn't say that.

TOM.   You implied it.

HARRY.   I meant, you're not the only one who does.

TOM.   What you're really saying is, the one person in this house that counts is *you.*

HARRY. If you don't like it, you know what to do.

TOM. What's that?

HARRY. Get out.

TOM. Do you want to know the one thing that's stopping me?

HARRY. No.

TOM. Mum. The thought of leaving her alone. . . in this dump. . . with you. . .

(HARRY *exits.*

TOM *throws down the paper, crosses to the sofa, turns on a transistor radio, sits and reads a magazine.*

The music continues. HARRY *comes back in.*)

HARRY. Your mother's in tears. A fine return we get. . . for the sacrifices we've made.

TOM. It was her that made the sacrifices, not you.

HARRY. To think. . . Men were dropped. . . parachuted behind enemy lines. . . to safeguard the future. So that the world would be a better place, for the next generation. Half a platoon, blown to pieces. . . the courage, the human sacrifice. . .

TOM. The biggest sacrifice she made. . . was marrying you.

(As he passes the transistor, HARRY *irritably turns it off.)*

HARRY. What do you know about marriage? How dare you talk to me about marriage? You don't show any sign of ever getting married.

TOM. Come out in spots, do you?

HARRY. You've never brought a girl back here.

TOM. That doesn't mean I haven't got one.

HARRY. Produce her. Bring her out of your hat. Go on. Surprise me.

TOM. I could have, for all you know.

HARRY. Why do we never see her, then?

TOM. You don't think I'd bring her here, do you?

To have you slobbering all over her?

HARRY.   You wouldn't know how to treat a girl, if you had one.

TOM.   Meaning you would. Sure, I can just see you. When you were my age. Walking along the prom, in your striped bathing costume. Rippling your muscles. Sticking out your chest. Or in the Pool, lording it over the small boys . . . showing off . . . diving in from the top board to impress her.

HARRY.   More than you'll ever achieve.

TOM.   Doing the crawl.

HARRY.   It wasn't the crawl.

TOM.   I thought that was what the wee cup was for.

HARRY.   The bloody breaststroke.

TOM.   The breaststroke. . . Oooh, weren't the girls lucky?

HARRY.   I swam for the Squadron. . . Broke the Squadron record.

TOM.   Pity you went to seed so soon.

HARRY.   What was that?

TOM.   Look at you!

HARRY.   Take a look at yourself. There isn't an ounce of manhood in you. You've no spunk.

(Pause.)

TOM.   Know what would serve you right? If I *did* have a girl. And was to get her into trouble. If I was to put her up the spout. That'd be one in the eye for you. That'd set the Tory hut talking.

HARRY.   If I even thought you could. . . You haven't got what it takes. You're still tied to mummy's apron-strings.

TOM.   Shut up.

HARRY.   Out at the pictures with Brian, then home to mummy. . .

TOM.   Good thing I know it's the drink that's talking.

HARRY. Wee jessie.

TOM. If I was to put a match to you, you'd go up in a blue light.

HARRY. A wee jessie. . . a sissie. . . a nancy-boy. . .

TOM. I'm the son of a lush. That's what I am.

HARRY. Bloody little pansy!

TOM. Take that back.

HARRY. Take back what you said to me. *(Pause)* Pansy!

TOM. Listen! Listen to me! I may not have a girl. But if I did, do you know what I wouldn't do? Listen to me! The one thing I wouldn't do. . . would be to take her round behind the Pool, in a little green van . . . and take advantage of her . . . a little green van, wasn't it? The windows all steamed up? And then . . . years later, throw it in her face.

(TOM *and* HARRY *both downstage.)*

HARRY. You were eavesdropping . . . you pipsqueak . . . You filthy . . . little . . . sneak . . .

TOM. Sticks and stones . . .

HARRY. I'll break every bone in your body.

TOM. No guts.

HARRY. I'll break you. I'll discredit you.

TOM. How!

HARRY. I'll discredit you. In your mother's eyes.

TOM. I wish it was you that had cancer.

(EDITH *has appeared in the doorway.*

HARRY *sees her.*

TOM *turns, makes some sound, and immediately exits.)*

EDITH. Harry . . .?

(HARRY *goes to the sideboard, lifts his empty glass. He turns.*

59

HARRY. It . . . it wasn't . . .

(HARRY *puts down the glass, grabs his jacket, pushes clumsily past her, and exits.*

EDITH *stands there.*

BLACKOUT

Scene 2

That night.

The conjuring table has been moved aside. The flower-bowl on the table. The curtains are drawn. The radiator is lit. The kitchen light is on. Otherwise the stage is in darkness.

A shadow is cast across the hatch. We hear the sound of a spoon in a cup. EDITH *comes into the room. She wears a dressing-gown; and looks attractive—almost youthful. She crosses towards the window, pulls one curtain aside, looks out.*

The front door closes, off.

TOM *comes into the room, tiptoes towards the hatch, turns and sees her in the shadow.*

TOM. What are you doing, in the dark?

EDITH. Come and sit down.

TOM. I'm going to my bed.

EDITH. No, you're not.

TOM. Is he in yet?

EDITH. No.

TOM. Can I have a cup of coffee?

EDITH. There's enough in the kettle.

(TOM *goes to the kitchen.* EDITH *puts on the standard lamp. She draws the dressing-gown round her.* TOM *comes in, with a mug of coffee.)*

What did you mean?

TOM. It was nothing to do with you.

EDITH.   I want to know what you meant.

TOM.   It affects him, not you.

EDITH.   It affects me too.

TOM.   How does it affect . . .?

EDITH.   You're not leaving this room, until you've told me.

TOM.   You don't think . . .

EDITH.   I don't know . . . what to think.

TOM.   Look . . .

EDITH.   What do you . . . expect me to think?

TOM.   You haven't been . . . sitting in here . . . Christ, you're wrong . . . It was right off the top of my head, that I . . . He goaded me . . . That's what . . . triggered it off. It . . . wasn't anything to do with you, at all . . .

EDITH.   You're lying.

TOM.   Honest, I'm not.

EDITH.   How am I to know that?

TOM.   I'm *not.*

EDITH.   How am I to know . . . the surgeon wasn't lying to me? That Harry hasn't been lying to me? Hasn't lied to me, all along? How am I to know, when you come out with a thing like that . . . in my hearing? How am I to know I'm not . . . being deceived? That I haven't been deceived, from the start? That something . . . something terrible . . . isn't being . . . hidden from me?

TOM.   I *can't* hide anything. I don't *know* anything.

EDITH.   Is that . . . the truth?

TOM.   It's the God's truth.

EDITH.   You'd say that . . . anyway.

TOM.   I wouldn't. How could I? I couldn't hide . . . that. Not from you. Look, can't you tell . . . from my eyes . . . that I'm not lying? I couldn't . . . look you straight in the eye . . . and not . . . Mum

61

(EDITH *moves away, sits.*)

Do you believe me?

EDITH. *(After a pause)* Yes Tom . . . I do. *(Half to herself)* I've no option . . . but to believe you . . .

TOM. I blurted it out, that's all . . . I never dreamed . . . Anyway it was him I was getting at, not you . . . *Him!*

EDITH. *(Whirls round)* Do you realise . . . what it has done to him?

TOM. I don't care.

EDITH. You what!

TOM. You . . . wouldn't understand . . . he humiliated me . . .

EDITH. So . . . you tried to humiliate him?

TOM. He asked for it. He *deserved* it.

(She rises fiercely.)

EDITH. Who do you think you are? To decide what he deserves? Who are you, to call him to account?

(But TOM *is silent. She speaks with real intensity.)*

I remember . . . he used to sit you on that mantel-piece . . . he used to walk this room with you in his arms . . . with *you,* over *his* shoulder . . . You were helpless, in his arms . . . And he was . . . proud of you . . . so proud . . . Now that you're stronger than he is, you try to humiliate him. Why? What has he done, to deserve that? He is older than you. And perhaps weaker. That does not entitle you . . . to take advantage of him. To deride him. To try and destroy . . . what is left of his self-respect. The last shreds . . . the vestiges . . . of his self-respect . . .

TOM. The last shreds. . . Exactly . . . He makes me . . . ashamed . . .

EDITH. The shame lies in your treatment of him. In the way you always seek to blacken him, to belittle him.

TOM. It's you . . . You always whitewash him.

(She controls herself.)

EDITH. Don't you understand? . . . Being married to
someone . . . means being aware of their . . . their
failings . . . And making allowances, for them . . .
Both ways . . . Your father . . . is no more fallible. . .
than most . . . Can't you see that?

TOM. You're defending him.

EDITH. It's my duty to defend him. And protect him.
When he's incapable of . . . defending himself.

TOM. Because he's always drunk?

EDITH. He is not always drunk. *(Pause)* He . . . has the
odd drink . . . To steady his nerves . . . When he's . . .
under pressure, at the office . . . You don't know
what it's like, for him . . . what he has to put up
with . . . from McCallum . . . all of them . . . It . . .
steadies his nerves . . . helps him . . . relax . . .

TOM. You won't admit it. You pretend not to notice.
Turn a blind eye. Why? Why do you . . . condone
it? Hoping it'll go away?

EDITH. All I can do. . . is try and help him. . . keep his
head . . . above water. . . *(Pause, then she turns
wildly on him)* I hope to God you never have a
son, who does to you what you have tried to do to
your father. Who humiliates you, the way you
have humiliated him. I hope your son . . . never
calls you . . . to account . . .

TOM. I hope I never do . . . to my son . . . what he
did . . . to me . . .

(Pause, then in a changed tone.)

I love you, Mum.

EDITH. So does your Father . . . love me.

TOM. How can he? When he said what he did? To
you? I overheard him, from the hall. Earlier this
evening . . .

EDITH. Tom!

TOM. I couldn't help it. I went out. And came back in
a few minutes later, slamming the door so that he'd
know I was there . . .

(Pause.)

EDITH. Couldn't you . . . have pretended . . . not to hear?

TOM. I did.

EDITH. Couldn't you have had the decency?

TOM. Who's talking about decency!

(EDITH cups her face in her hands. TOM does not know how to comfort her. He takes the cup and mug to the hatch, leaves them there. She gives a racking sob, and subsides on the sofa. He hesitates, about to leave the room.)

EDITH. Tom . . . Wait . . .

(He stops.)

TOM. There's no point . . .

EDITH. You must let me explain . . .

TOM. There's no need . . .

EDITH. Please . . . *(She rises, crosses centre-stage).* There's something . . . I must tell you. For your own sake. Before . . . your father comes in. And before you judge him . . . and me . . . too strictly. We met . . . Harry and I . . . you know this . . . *(She sits)* We met during the War . . . It seems ages ago now . . . the air-raids and ration-books . . . Anyway, I'm not going to try and justify what occurred . . . I simply want you to know . . . Your father was in the Air Force. I was doing auxiliary nursing. He came in to visit a friend, who had been wounded and flown home. To Blighty. Anyway, we saw one another several times. When he returned to France, we exchanged letters. Then I saw him when he came home on leave. We wanted to get married. But somehow there wasn't an opportunity. You could say we were . . . unofficially engaged. Anyway, what happened . . . happened. I'm not . . . trying to defend our action, Tom . . . All I'm saying is . . . it wasn't a . . . chance encounter, anything of that sort . . . what you maybe imagined . . . We desperately loved one another . . . and wanted to

64

... belong to one another. Don't be ... too
severe ... on us.

TOM.   Look, it doesn't matter to me. Whether you
were married or not. So long as I was ... on the
right side of the blanket, when the time came.
Even then ... look, to hell ... why should it
matter to me? Whether you were in love or not?
I mean ... I could be ... for all you know ... all
he knows ... I could be having it off every other
night. Couldn't I? I could have them queueing
up for it. *(Gasping)* Christ, I could be having it
away all the time. Stamina permitting. That
Swedish bit up the Terrace ... I could be screwing
her on the side ... I could be taking the pants
off her in here, even ... On this very sofa. Right
here!

EDITH.   But you're not, Tom ... are you?

TOM.   *(Pause)* I wish I bloody was!

(TOM *sits.*)

EDITH.   I hadn't ... quite finished, Tom ... what I
was going to tell you. Wait, it's important. Before
I met your father ... there was someone else.

(As TOM's *jaw drops:)*

He was a family friend. A flight lieutenant. Our
families were friendly ... his and mine. They'd
made their minds up that we were suited. Indeed
we were very fond ... of each other. In a purely
... romantic way ... I mean, there was never
anything ... remotely physical ... to it ... He
was a bomber pilot. I remember I had his photo
on my dressing-table, at home. Then one day, we
received news ... that he'd been shot down ...
over the Rhine. In a raid. He ... was awarded
the D.F.C. Posthumously. His mother insisted ...
I keep the medal ... because he'd told her he
was going to marry me, once it was all over. That
... and some of his letters ... are what Harry
found ... while I was in hospital. I'd never
mentioned them, to him ... There seemed no
point. I don't ... even know why I bothered to
keep them ... except ... *(She shrugs, continues)*

65

Harry knew about him, at the time. Knew he'd
. . . been lost . . . And I think he was always
afraid I'd married him . . . on the rebound . . .
something like that. It wasn't true. . . but he was
afraid . . . he was second-best. *(She looks at him)*
You see your father never flew, Tom . . .

TOM.   How could he . . . be parachuted . . . if he . . .?

EDITH.   I know, dear . . . But he couldn't. He failed
his medical. His ears . . . a result of his
swimming . . .

TOM.   But . . .

EDITH.   That only . . . made it worse . . . for him . . .
Anyway, when he came home, that last leave . . .
rightly or wrongly . . . I had to . . . give myself
to him. He needed me, Tom. That seemed all that
mattered. He loved me . . . And I was afraid . . .
that if I didn't . . . he might be sent back . . .
and be posted missing, and then I'd have nothing
. . . nothing at all . . .

(Long pause
EDITH *wipes here eyes.)*

Would you mind . . . getting me a glass of water
. . . please . . .

(TOM *goes to the kitchen.* EDITH *crosses
wearily to the sofa, sits.* TOM *brings her a glass
of water. She sips, hands him back the glass,
which he puts down.* EDITH *reclines on the sofa.
Pause.)*

TOM.   And now . . . after all those years . . .*(He sits
beside her. Pause.)* Anyway, the important thing
is . . . you've a clean sheet.

EDITH.   Yes, dear . . . a clean sheet.

(Pause.)

TOM.   The . . . surgeon told you, did he?

EDITH.   Yes, dear.

TOM.   When?

EDITH.   This morning.

TOM. Before you left hospital?

EDITH. Mmm.

TOM. Dad was told?

EDITH. What, dear?

TOM. Was Dad told? This morning?

EDITH. Yes, of course.

(EDITH *moves her head wearily.*)

TOM. He didn't tell me. He left me . . . to wonder
whether . . . He kept me in the dark, intentionally . . .
Who does he think he is! I'll show him up . . .
reveal him in his true colours . . . for what he is.
Making your life . . . a misery. He's not fit to . . .
(He rises, lifts the silver cup from the mantelpiece.)
For the breaststroke. All he has to show for
himself. After swimming through life . . . all he
has left behind is a wee cup . . . and a trail of
bubbles . . . a trail of silver bubbles . . . bursting on
the surface . . . *(At the mirror)* Adds columns of
figures all day, eyes up the miniskirts . . . then home
at night to stick patterns in an album, for pin
money . . . and all the time, he's canned . . . he's
half-jaked . . . It's my nerves, doctor, they've been
troubling me again . . . Oh thanks, doctor, that'll
work wonders . . . And the same to you!

*(He raises the cup as in a toast, pretends to drink.
He crosses the room.)*

Putting on the big act . . . kidding himself . . . And
all the time, underneath, there's nothing . . . sweet
damn all . . . He'll go through the remainder of his
days . . . the remainder of his life . . . pub-crawling
and arse-licking . . . till he ends up . . . in No Man's
Land . . . nowhere-a-bloody-t-all . . . But before he
goes, I'll pay him back . . . for what he's done. For
the hurt he's caused . . .

(He glances across at EDITH. *She appears to be
asleep. He crosses to the conjuring table, lifts a
chiffon.)*

One night years ago, I came in late. And as I was
passing your bedroom door I heard you crying,

and him talking to you. You were moaning and
sobbing. His voice became higher and higher. I
wanted to burst in. But I was afraid to. There was
nothing I could do. I stood there, imagining him
striking you, tearing at you, beating you . . . Then
it seemed to pass . . . and I went to my room . . .
and tried to sleep . . . And I remember . . . I dreamed
there was to be a tourney. For the hand of the
fairest maiden in the Field. Between him and me. As
in medieval days, fiery steeds, jousts and cloth of
gold. Trumpets sounding, banners flared, the white
kerchief falling . . . *(He lets the chiffon drift to the
ground.)* Dew shimmering, under the stallions'
hooves . . . In the glittering air, my ascending axe . . .
My plume tilting, the trees enamel, the sun a ball
of fire. The crowd swaying and cheering, urging us
on. Our breath like blooms of steam, as we thrust
and thundered. He ducks, but I have him. Then
round and again . . . He dodges, but I have him.
His limbs flail, in the heat. His fingers at my throat.
But I twist him and turn. I lift him, and lever, and
arch him down. I lock him and swing. Another to
the groin. I have him, and stamp him and clamp
him down.

(His feet stamping. His shadow moving.)

I smash him and stamp him, I ram him down. *(He
has started to stamp his feet. This reaches its
climax)* I drum him . . . and drown him . . . I
drum him . . . down . . . Till at last . . . the Beast
. . . is dead!

*(He seems in a state of exhaustion. His head
forward, bemused. At the same time, triumphant.
Suddenly he changes his posture and his tone:)*

Milords, Ladies and Gennemen. . . the undisputed
champion, in the red corner, with a bellylock,
two Boston crabs and a final decapitation: the
Kelvinside Killer . . . Tommy Kid Rankin!

*(He raises both arms, as if to acknowledge the
cheers. Again he alters his stance and tone:)*

And now for the Prize !!!

*(Adopting a Groucho Marx stoop, eyebrows
working, and puffing an imaginary ciagar, he*

crosses to the sofa. Still doing his impression
TOM *steps up on the sofa. He exhales, looks down
at* EDITH.)

Dear Lady, give me your hand.

*(Transferring his imaginary cigar to his own left
hand, he adds:)*

You can have it back tomorrow.

*(With his right hand he reaches towards her. As
he bends down he loses his balance. He falls on
top of her, spreadeagles her.*

EDITH *screams loudly.*

HARRY *appears in the doorway.)*

HARRY.   What in God's name . . .

*(He switches on the room light.
TOM tries to rise. HARRY moves towards him.)*

If he's harmed a hair of your head . . .

EDITH.   Harry . . . let me explain . . .

TOM *has risen.* EDITH *rises, steps between*
HARRY *and* TOM. HARRY *thrusts her aside.
This sparks off* TOM.)

TOM.   You're dead! I've killed you!

HARRY.   What was that!

EDITH.   I can explain.

TOM.   Beast!

HARRY.   I'll teach you a lesson . . . you won't
forget. Edith, go to your room.

EDITH.   Harry, please . . .

HARRY.   *(To* TOM) You ought to be horse-whipped.

TOM.   The Beast . . . is . . . dead . . .

HARRY.   Shut your mouth!

TOM.   Get to fuck!

HARRY.   You've besmirched my house.

(HARRY *turns on his heel and leaves the room.*)

EDITH.   Go to bed before he comes back. Quickly, Tom
. . . for my sake . . . I'll explain that you were
carried away.

*(But HARRY comes back. He has a thick leather
belt, which he ripples through his fingers.)*

HARRY.   Go to bed, Edith.

EDITH.   I will Harry. If you'll come with me.

HARRY.   This is . . . between him and me. *(Pause)*
I'm waiting.

EDITH.   Harry!

HARRY.   I said I'm waiting.

(She crosses to the door, but does not exit.)

(To TOM) Are you ready to take your medicine?

TOM.   You don't understand.

HARRY.   I don't have to. Get down there.

TOM.   Don't be stupid. It's you I'm worried about. You
might not . . . be able to take it.

HARRY.   Whining won't help.

TOM.   Dad . . .

HARRY.   Don't say you're yellow?

(Quickly TOM *lies on the sofa, head towards*
HARRY.)

Put your hands underneath. I don't want to
damage your wrists.

*(TOM obeys, but keeping his arms in a position
that will enable him to spring up, if need be.)*

EDITH.   Harry, you don't know what you're doing . . .
He's your son . . .

HARRY.   I told you I'd make a man of him . . . if it
killed me . . .

TOM.   Get on with it, then.

EDITH.   No, Harry.

HARRY. Keep back. (HARRY *thrusts* EDITH *aside.*)

TOM. Don't say it's you that's yellow? Now it comes to
the bit? Don't say you can't go through with it?
Why not use the buckled end? No guts? I know . . .
it's a thrill you're after. You really fancy me, that
it? Maybe it's you that's the pansy. Want me to take
my trousers down? Fancy a bit of brown?

(HARRY *lashes out blindly with the belt.*)

HARRY. *(Screams)* Filth!!!

(TOM *throws himself from the sofa, away from*
HARRY.

EDITH *rushes forward, tries to come between*
them. HARRY *pushes past her. She loses her*
balance, goes down—taking the flex of the lamp
with her.

The light goes out: leaving the room lit from the
hall and the kitchen, and the red glow of the
radiator casting grotesque shadows.

HARRY *lashes out at* TOM. TOM *evades him. At*
the sideboard TOM *grabs a little brass bell. He*
waves it above his head.)

TOM. Unclean! Unclean! Unclean!

EDITH. For the love of God . . .

(HARRY *blunders towards* TOM. *Again*
EDITH *tries to come between them.* HARRY, *in*
striking out at TOM *hits her with the belt. She*
screams. TOM *freezes.* HARRY's *momentum*
takes him to the table: he leans against it,
breathless.)

TOM. Where's the big hero now? The big War hero?
Women and children, is that all you're fit to fight?
What did you really do in the War, daddy? Where
did you fly to? What have you got to show for it?
A wee cup, for the breaststroke. Where are your
medals? *(Pause)* Where is *your* D.F.C?

(HARRY *gapes at* TOM *for a moment, then at*
EDITH. *He sways forward, then his legs buckle*
beneath him. He crumples to the floor. EDITH
rushes to him.)

EDITH. Harry . . . Harry . . . ? *(To* TOM) Get his
pills. From beside his bed.

(TOM *exits.* EDITH *cradles* HARRY, *strokes
his forehead.)*

You'll be all right, Harry . . . Don't say anything
. . . Don't try . . . to speak . . . *(She looks up as*
TOM *comes in.)* There's some water in that glass.

(TOM *hands her the pills, then the glass.*
EDITH *gives the pills to* HARRY—*putting them
in his mouth, and helping him to sip a little
water.)*

TOM. Is he . . . Will he be . . . ?

(EDITH *hands him the glass. He holds it
awkwardly.)*

HARRY. Tom, I . . . Edith . . .

EDITH. Sssh, dear . . . everything's going to be . . .
all right . . . Don't . . . worry . . .

HARRY. You . . . told him . . .

EDITH. I had to, Harry. He had to know . . .

HARRY. Why?

EDITH. It's better . . . he should know . . .

HARRY. How can he . . . ever respect me . . . now,
Edith?

EDITH. He'll respect you . . . all the more . . .

(Pause. HARRY's *breathing.* TOM *sorts the
flex, lights the lamp. The brightness momentarily blinds* HARRY. *He looks round at* TOM,
then at EDITH.)

HARRY. What was he doing? What . . . were you doing?
What . . . ?

EDITH. The boy was playing the fool, Harry. He
didn't mean any harm. It was only . . .

HARRY. When I came in . . . it wasn't the boy I
saw . . . It wasn't the boy I wanted . . . to
destroy . . . It was someone I've been . . .
trying to live up to . . . all those years . . . knowing

72

I could never . . . succeed . . . All my married
life . . . I've been . . . second-best . . .

EDITH.   You're wrong. I kept them, the medal, and the
letters . . . simply because I hadn't the heart to
throw them out.

HARRY.   Then why keep them a secret?

EDITH.   Not a secret. They just lay there. In a drawer.
I wish you'd discovered them years ago, if it'd
have set your mind at rest. Harry, I love you . . .
You . . . For what you are . . .

HARRY.   How can you?

EDITH.   I sometimes wonder. But I do.

(Pause.)

HARRY.   Where's the boy?

EDITH.   Don't . . . exhaust yourself, dear . . . You'll
need all your energy . . .

(TOM *steps forward, helps to support him.)*

TOM.   I'm sorry, Dad . . .

EDITH.   Lie down here, Harry . . .

HARRY.   Thanks.

(For a moment HARRY *stands unsupported.
He looks at* TOM, *sways slightly.)*

EDITH.   Will you be all right, Harry?

HARRY.   Sure. Nothing the matter . . . with me . . .
that a good night's rest . . . won't put right . . .
(He looks at TOM) I'm . . .

(EDITH *and* TOM *help him to lie on the sofa.)*

Don't . . . worry . . . Everything's going to be . . .
hunkey-dorey . . .

(His eyes are closed.)

EDITH.   Get a rug, Tom.

(TOM *brings a travelling rug from the sideboard.*
EDITH *wraps it carefully round* HARRY.)

TOM.   Will he really . . . be all right?

(TOM *puts the bell back in place; rolls up the belt, puts it aside.*)

EDITH.   I've failed him. I haven't loved him enough, Tom . . . Over the years . . . I haven't . . . shown my love for him . . .

TOM.   That's not the same. They're two different things.

EDITH.   What's the use of loving someone . . . if you don't *show* it? We all care . . . but how often do we *show* it? How often have I shown it? To your father?

(*The doorbell rings. It takes a moment to sink in. EDITH stands, stricken. The doorbell again.*)

EDITH.   It'll be Ella . . .

TOM.   This time of night?

EDITH.   It . . . isn't really late.

TOM.   I can't answer. She'll come back tomorrow.

EDITH.   She'll know we're still up.

TOM.   Stuff her! And her . . . bloody yoghourt!

(*The doorbell again.*)

EDITH.   You'll have to answer, Tom.

TOM.   All right. But let her put one foot inside that door . . . I'll . . . slam it on her bloody fingers.

(TOM *exits.* EDITH *tidies the rug, round* HARRY.

Voices off.

EDITH *takes a deep breath, touches her hair. Front door closes, off.*

Silence.

TOM *appears alone in the doorway, stands awkwardly.*)

Mum . . .

74

(Pause. ELLA appears.)

EDITH. *(Makes an effort)* Hello, Ella . . . Harry's . . .

(Something in ELLA's manner silences her. ELLA comes into the room, like someone trying to find her bearings.)

ELLA. I'm that sorry, Edith . . . I didn't want to trouble you . . . But there was nowhere else . . . I could go . . .

EDITH. What is it? Is it Frank?

(ELLA nods.)

He's taken another of his turns, is that it? Tell me, Ella . . . Are you all right, Ella?

ELLA. I'll have to . . . hang on to something, so I will . . .

EDITH. You don't mean . . .

ELLA. He's . . . dead. I think . . . he's dead.

(Frozen silence.)

EDITH. *(To TOM)* Phone for the Doctor, Tom and get my coat.

(TOM exits.)

I'll come down with you . . . Pray God you're wrong.

ELLA. It's real enough, Edith. God help me . . . Many's the time I've prayed for him . . . to be taken out of his misery . . . to be . . . released . . . But I never dreamt . . . I can't take it in, so I can't . . .

EDITH. What happened, Ella? Here, sit down . . .

ELLA. I'll be all right . . . He had one of his wee turns, early this evening . . . So I packed him off to bed. Later on, after he'd been sleeping for a wee while, I thought I heard him cry out. So I went through. There he was, bolt upright, clutching the sheets . . . the sweat running down him . . . And he started going on about . . . those vibrations . . . Said he could feel them, stronger than ever . . . Worse, than ever before . . . And more than vibrations, this time . . . a stamping, he said . . . a stamping,

75

and with it, the sound of . . . a bell . . . He said
it . . . it must be . . . some kind of Judgment on
him.

(TOM *has returned, in time to hear this.*)

TOM. No!

(ELLA *turns, looks at* TOM. *Then at* HARRY. *She
seems unable to focus.*)

ELLA. There was a funny smell in here, earlier on, like
celery. But it seems to have gone now.

(EDITH *lays a hand on* ELLA's *arm. Pause, and:*)

All of a sudden, he toppled forward and the blood
came rushing up and all the life . . . seemed to
stream out of him . . . I did what I could but he
was . . . he was just like . . . he was just like a log,
so he was . . . I still can't credit what's happened . . .
I can't take it in . . .

(EDITH *takes* ELLA *in her arms.*)

EDITH. We'll go down . . . and see what we can do . . .
And I'll . . . make you a cup of tea . . .

ELLA. You're . . . a real tower of strength, Edith . . . so
you are . . .

EDITH. Come along . . .

TOM. Is there . . . nothing I can do?

EDITH. No, you stay here, son . . . He enjoys your
visits, Frank does . . . having the odd crack, now
and then . . . No, you wait here . . . I'm that sorry,
on your mother's first night home . . . Frank . . .
Frank . . .

EDITH. You've been . . . a wonderful wife to him,
Ella . . . all those years . . .

ELLA. No . . . You mustn't say that. I can't bear it.

(She is on the point of breaking down.)

EDITH. Come along . . . gently does it . . .

(EDITH *helps* ELLA *to her feet and guides her to
the door.*

TOM *steps forward hesitantly.*)

ELLA.   You wait here, son . . . With your
father. Your mother'll be back directly . . . God
help me when it hits me, Edith . . . when it . . .
sinks in . . .

EDITH.   Yes, you wait here, Tom . . . I'll be back . . .
directly . . .

(ELLA *exits, followed by* EDITH.

TOM *stands in the doorway.*

Pause, and we hear the front door close, off.

TOM *listens for a moment.*

He turns, looks across at HARRY.

He comes forward.

Slowly to Black.)

CURTAIN

THE MAN IN THE GREEN MUFFLER

A Play in One Act

CHARACTERS

Sid
Man

Pavement. Railings.
On the railings, gaudy drawings in chalk and crayon.

As the lights come up SID *is on his knees, drawing. At last he rises, dissatisfied. With a wet cloth, he rubs out part of what he has done. Throwing the cloth behind him, he starts over again.*

A MAN *enters. Tall, bulky. He wears an overcoat, carries a case. After watching* SID *for a few moments the* MAN *crosses towards him.* SID *does not notice. The* MAN *stands behind him, very close.* SID *lays aside one stick of chalk, continues with another. Then he feels for the cloth, and touches the* MAN's *foot.*

SID. About time.

> *(Without turning round, he feels for the cloth, finds it and carries on.)*

All I can say.

(No reply)

Some time I've had. I can tell you. With those hills. Getting the right shade. The skyline. Trees against the skyline. Bad enough at the best of times.

(No response)

Bad enough. Without you standing in my light. Makes me . . .

> *(Something makes him break off. He turns his head, examines the* MAN's *shoes at very close range.)*

Where'd you get that pair? Not your usual.

> *(Still no response. Very slowly,* SID *raises his eyes. He studies the* MAN's *turn-ups, then his knees, then his coat at eye-level.*

81

Finally SID *jerks his head back, so that he sees (for the first time) the* MAN's *face from below.)*

Bloody hell . . . you're . . . you're not . . . It isn't. . .

(SID *scrambles to his feet. He stares at the* MAN. *The* MAN *gazes back, steadily.)*

Eh?

(The MAN *turns his back, walks to the railings, studies* SID's *work.)*

Hey you!

MAN. Right about the sky, ask me. The skyline. Trees don't seem quite right. What's the word?

SID. You what?

MAN. Indeterminate, that's it. Too indeterminate.

SID. Creeping up on me like that. Enough to give a bloke the shivers. When you're not . . .

MAN. Not what?

SID. Not him.

MAN. Not who?

SID. Who are you? I thought you were him. He always stands behind me like that. When I'm at it. Normally earlier than this. That's why I thought he was late. Only it turned out . . . it was you. Anyway, you can't stay there.

MAN. Free country.

SID. You're on his pitch.

MAN. Whose?

SID. That's what I'm trying to tell you. Albert's.

MAN. I see. It disturbs you. That I'm not Albert?

SID. Doesnt disturb me. But it'll disturb you, if he comes along and catches you there. He's late already.

MAN. So I gather. Do I look like him? Is that why you took me for him?

SID. Not took. *Mis*took. That was before I saw you.

82

Second I set eyes on . . . clapped eyes on you, I
knew. Second I saw the shoes. Albert doesn't wear
shoes like that. Suede. Not his cup of tea. Nothing
like you. Not remotely similar. Not your build, for
a start. He's like a bantam-cock. You carry too
much weight, for a kick-off. Facial similarity?
Nope. *(Pause)* Well? *(Pause)* You going to blow?

MAN.   I'm interested to see how you finish that one.
Try high-lighting the hills, eh?

SID.   Have it your own way. Only don't blame me, if
Albert . . .

MAN.   If Albert what?

SID.   If he doesn't take to you. When he comes.

MAN.   He won't be coming.

SID.   Your own funeral. What did you say?

MAN.   He won't be coming. I'm standing in for him.

SID.   Why didn't you say? Straight off? Saved a lot of
trouble. You a friend of his?

MAN.   You could say we're pretty close. Have been.

SID.   Any friend of Albert's . . . *(His expression changes)*
Hey, how do I know this is true? How can I trust
you?

MAN.   Just have to, friend.

SID.   How am I to know—?

MAN.   I've got his stuff, haven't I? See for yourself!

(The MAN *opens his case, which turns into a tray
with a strap for going round the neck. On the tray
are jumping-beans. The* MAN *puts on the tray, as*
SID *watches.)*

His kit. Okay, friend?

SID.   Sure . . . only . . . what do you mean, stand in?
(No reply) Albert can move them a deal faster than
that. *(No reply)* That was what worried me, at the
start. That you might be trying to . . . to imper-
sonate him. Had your guts for garters, in that case.
Anyway, I've no option. But to take your word for
it. But no funny business. I've eyes on the back of
my head.

(SID *gets down on his knees, starts drawing. He shoots a glance at the* MAN, *but the* MAN *is ignoring him, all his attention being apparently on the beans which jump to and fro as the tray is tilted.*)

No skin off my nose!

(He continues drawing.)

MAN.   Draw from memory, do you?

SID.   Course I ruddy do.

MAN.   I hoped you were.

SID.   Otherwise the ruddy railings'd be in the picture. Wouldn't they?

MAN.   It was the friendly atmosphere of this corner, Albert said, that always impressed him. Endeared itself to him.

SID.   *(Automatically)* Sure. . .

MAN.   You got on well together, you and him?

SID.   Course we do. Couldn't have shared adjoining pitches all these years, if we didn't get along together. Stands to reason.

MAN.   He said you were always . . . good for morale. Always ready with the cheery word . . .

SID.   Albert said that?

(The MAN *nods.* SID *looks with disbelief. Then he decides to live up to the image.)*

Well, I do my best to keep his pecker up. You know, the odd story . . . gag or two . . .

MAN.   Tell me one.

SID.   I . . . well . . . look, I haven't all day . . . but . . . well, later . . . as soon as I've finished . . . *(and he deflates)*

MAN.   I'll tell you one, in that case.

SID.   No.

MAN.   Albert said he told you gags too.

84

SID. You be a . . . stand-in. But you're not Albert."
Sorry. I've got to get on . . .

MAN. This man goes into the pub, and goes up to the
bar, and says (*speaks through his nose*) 'pint of
beer, please . . .'

SID. I've heard it. Albert told me it. Ages ago.

MAN. Bet you laughed.

SID. Course. He's good at telling jokes.

MAN. Pretty thick, you and Albert?

SID. Best of mates. Goes back years, our association.
Relationship. One of the best, take it from me.
Salt of the earth. I remember some nights with
Albert. Him on the old joanna. Or a touch of the
old razzle-dazzle on the paper and comb.

MAN. Good company?

SID. The best.

MAN. No malice?

SID. Wouldn't hurt a fly if it belted him one in the
kisser. Always ready for a bit of fun.

MAN. Thought he was in trouble, a few times.

SID. Only because of some prank that backfired. Take
the time of the teddy-bears. No, wait a minute . . .
you see, he had this idea . . . He managed to get
hold of . . . don't ask me how he did it . . . some
old walkie-talkie sets . . .

MAN. Where from?

SID. And he flogged all of them but one. And you
know what he did? He set himself up in an old
workman's hut. Just off the Old Kent Road it
was . . . set himself up . . .

MAN. What's this to do with teddy-bears?

SID. If you'd wait. He set up his walkie-talkie centre.
Then he got hold of a couple of hundred surplus
teddy-bears. And fitted them up. Sort of radar
system. And he had them walking up and down
the pavement, on display. Sold dozens of them.

The Talking Teddy-Bear Show, he called it. But he went bust. Somehow the wires got crossed, and he started coming up on the taxi wavelengths. Then one day he came over on Top of the Pops, and he had to make a run for it. Course, his training went back years.

MAN. And you've known him all that long?

SID. Sure. The parties we've been to, times we've been through ... I remember once, near Bristol it was—

MAN. Yes, he's told me about some of your outings, together.

SID. Yeah? (*Pause*) Go on.

MAN. One or two in particular.

SID. Meaning?

MAN. In the old Riley ...

SID. What about it? Don't know what you're—

MAN. Not what Albert said.

SID. I drove him around, sure, but that was the end of it.

MAN. Let's change the subject. *(Sharply)* How was he with kids?

SID. Regular Santa Claus. Any chance he could get. Loved them. Everyone's favourite uncle ...

MAN. Ballocks!

SID. If you don't bloody believe me, why ask?

MAN. Ballocks!

SID. Mind what you're saying about—

MAN. If Albert went after a kid, it was with only one thing in mind.

SID. That's a lie. That's maligning him.

MAN. Out in that old Riley ... cruising ... up and down ... behind the bandstand ...

SID. He told you about the bandstand?

MAN. Who else?

SID. What about it?

MAN. Few things.

SID. Look, mister, nothing happened.

MAN. Not what *he* said.

SID. He's a good sort, Albert. I mean, maybe under
stress, now and again, he acts a bit peculiar . . .
know what I mean . . . what I'm getting at . . .
don't put too much store by . . . What did he say?
(No reply) I know what you're doing. Trying to
trick me. Lull me into a false . . . to betray
Albert . . . Let me tell you this, you've had your
chips. You'll worm nothing out of me . . . I'll tell
you nothing about Albert . . . not one solitary,
single, stricken iota. And if he told you he'd done
anything, all I can say is . . . he must've been
having you on.

MAN. He didn't say he'd done anything. *(Pause)* He
said *you* had!

(Moment's silence. Then:)

SID. The bastard. He said I . . . what? What did he say?
(And he approaches the MAN)

MAN. Plenty.

SID. Bloody lies. Look, all I did was . . . drive the car
for him . . .

MAN. And look on, while—

SID. Yes. No.

MAN. How could he be lying? If he's the fine fellow
you made out? A few minutes ago?

SID. I was laying it on a bit. You know, gilding the
lily . . . I didn't realise he'd let the cat out of the
bag.

MAN. So there's something to let out?

SID. He told you there was, didn't he? Isn't that what
you said?

MAN. Go on!

SID. You'll get bugger all out of me. It was none of my

87

doing. I only went along, 'cos I was scared of him. . .
he had me by the . . .

MAN.   Come off it.

SID.   You've no right to—

MAN.   I want to know which of you was responsible.

SID.   What for?

MAN.   You know bloody well, friend.

SID.   Sure. . . he was. It was his idea. . . I never touched
her. . . all I did was lift her. . . you know. . . it was
Albert. . . and you say he told you it was me? The
lying bastard. He's always had it in for me. Know
that? For a fact. He's been biding his time. I
wouldn't go in as deep as him. He's been waiting. . .
(He changes tone) Look, what's it to do with you?
You a dick?

MAN.   Nope.

SID.   Let him face the music.

MAN.   He has.

SID.   How come? He'll lay into you for this. When he
comes.

MAN.   You're forgetting, I'm standing in for him.

SID.   He's still bound to look in. How about you and
me doing a deal, eh? Here. . . what was that about
him facing the music?

MAN.   What I say.

SID.   Come off it! You're trying to—

MAN.   Albert's dead.

SID.   Trying to scare me. Put the shits up me. . . What
was that? Who's dead?

MAN.   Albert. Aren't you sorry?

SID.   Why sorry? Dance on his grave, soon as look at him.
All he ever did for me! And as for what he must've
told you. . . Hey, you're having me on. . . one
minute you tell me he's dead, the minute before
you've been telling me how he spilt all those beans. . .

88

it doesn't fit in. . . it's inconsistent. . . you. . . it's
all a put-up job between you and him. . . a trick, to
get me to tell you it was him, so that he could get
me for it. . . maim me. . . the lengths he'd go to. . .
but when he comes, he won't find me. . . 'cos I
won't be here. . . I've a mind of my own, you
know. . . not bound to his whims. . . *(But he
becomes more and more hesitant)* You're having
me on, aren't you? Albert sent you, to put the
wind up me, that it? Bit of a laugh? The old April
Fool bit, eh? *(Pause)* Well? Wasn't it?

(But the MAN *shakes his head.)*

Okay, you've had your laugh. . . now you can go. . .
you'd better go. . . because Albert always has the
last laugh. . . and he'll have it on you too. . . I
mean, he can be. . . well, erratic. . . even if he did
tell you something, he's liable to go back on it. . .
my outburst, it wasn't warranted. . . but you got
me on the raw. . . all those suggestions. . . Look,
why won't you go. . . and leave us alone?

(But the MAN *has taken off the tray, and sat
beside the railings.)*

We could have the law on you. Scandal. Slander.
We'll stick together, you wait and see. . .

(The MAN *simply shakes his head.)*

What is it you want?

MAN.   You don't understand. Albert will not be coming.
Albert has kicked the bucket. Or had it kicked from
under him, you could say.

SID.   Look, it'll soon be. . . what was that? What do
you. . .? Can't you be more specific?

MAN.   Sounds pretty specific to me.

SID.   How, had it. . . kicked from under him? Look, are
you trying to tell me. . . to get me to believe. . .
accept the fact that. . .

(The MAN *nods his head, slowly.* SID *gapes at
him.)*

He was in the prime of. . . You're having me on!

(The MAN *shakes his head.)*

SID. I don't get it. You said you were his stand-in. Where?

MAN. Here.

SID. But. . . a stand-in's a temporary thing.

MAN. This time it's permanent.

SID. He's had stand-ins before. Like that time I
mentioned. . . the teddy-bears. . . or if he's in the
clink. . . that's giving away no secrets, everyone
knows. . . not maligning him. . . wouldn't do that. . .
specially if he's. . . gone. . . he'd hear me. . .
everything I say. . . everything I've been saying
about him. . . and he'll. . . he'd be waiting for me. . .
when my time comes. . . Look, if it'll help any, I'll
come clean. What he said was right. It was me. If
that's how you want it. Only I wasn't responsible.
You see, I have these turns. When. . . no warning. . .
everything goes. . . a kind of a haze over everything,
red and orange, then mauve. . . and as if there was
this great thundering voice, thundering yet in a sort
of echoing whisper. . . that tells me what to do. . .
like God's voice, only it can't be, because of the
sort of things it tells me to do. . . but I can't
disobey, it's not in my power. . . I try to fight it
off. . . that's why I rely on him, he helps me to
fight it off. . . only now and then, it's too strong
for us. . . and everything gets out of control. . .
snaps. . . I need him, to help me. . . I need Albert. . .

MAN. You'll have to put up with me, from now on.

SID. It won't be the same.

MAN. Am I so unlike him? *(Pause)* Describe him to me?

SID. It's all. . . everything's slipping. . . he isn't clear,
any longer. . . it's all. . . crumbling. . .

MAN. You must have some picture of him. . . of what
he was like?

SID. I'm trying. . . but. . . you see, I only find it easy
to describe things when they're in front of me. . .
that's why it's hard for me to draw from memory. . .
I keep putting in the railings, getting things wrong. . .
the trees, the skyline. . . he used to help me get

90

them right. . . but I remember him *for* things,
rather than *as* anything. . .

MAN.   You don't recall how he looked? You're a
painter. You remember the colours?

SID.   He had a ruddy complexion, not pale, like yours. . .
and he wore black shoes. . . and he. . . he had
bronchitis. . . every November it would come on
him, cough his guts up, like a vacuum-cleaner. . .
and there was always his muffler. . . he had a green
muffler, a huge green muffler. . . year in, year out. . .
twice round his neck and then hanging loose. . .
that's all I can remember. He's just a man. . . in a
green muffler. . . after what you've said. . . The
rest has gone. . . I don't know if he was good to me
or not, or whether I liked him or not. . . You said. . .
If what you say is true, how. . .?

(The MAN *rises)*

MAN.   You could say he was found. . . hanging. . .

SID.   Albert. . . hanged himself?

MAN.   Did I say that?

SID.   I thought you meant. . .

MAN.   You feeling all right?

SID.   Whose side are you on?

MAN.   Yours. No reason why we shouldn't get on, is
there? That I can see?

SID.   You knew him? Intimately?

MAN.   You could say we were. . . very close. . . latterly.

SID.   Tell me. . . how did he. . . did it. . . if he was. . .
like you said? What means. . .?

MAN.   Better not to go into. . . things like that.

SID.   Was the scarf. . . had it anything. . .?

(The MAN *nods his head.* SID *screws his face up,
in silence. Silence, then:)*

MAN.   Best to remember the old days, before things
turned sour.

*(*SID *nods his head.)*

Stories, you said? Good at telling gags? How about
me trying one on you? To see whether you've
heard it? *(No reply)* How about this one. There
was this man on the top deck of a bus. Across the
passage was another man, who got more and more
agitated, until he leaned forward and tapped the
man in front of him on the shoulder and said:
(With a speech blockage) 'Exc — c — cuse me, but
is is this the st — t — top for the Bot — t — tanic
Gardens?' But the bloke in front didn't move a
muscle. So the poor fellow had another go: 'Could
you t — t — tell me if this is the st — top for the
Bot — t — anics?' Still no reply. So the man across
the passage said, yes it was the right stop. And the
fellow got up and just made it, before the bus
started off again. And the man who'd helped out
waited until his stop came, and as he got up to
leave the bus he said pretty pointedly to the man
in front: 'You might have been civil enough to tell
that poor chap it was the right stop for him,
instead of ignoring him like that.' And the bloke in
front turned round, and looked at him for a
moment, and then said: 'Do you think I
w — w — wanted my bloody f — f —face kicked
in?!'

(A pause. SID *giggles nervously.)*

That better, then? More like old times?

(The MAN *lifts the tray, puts the strap round his
neck.*

SID *watches for a moment, then turns and looks
down at his own paintings. But instead of starting
drawing straight away, he straightens a pair of
pictures on the railings. He giggles again, and steps
back.*

The MAN *has tightened the strap, and straightened
the tray.*

Now he crosses, to stand behind SID—*in the same
position as at the start of the play.)*

MAN. Yes, it's the skyline, right enough. . . Not enough
definition. . .

(SID giggles nervously)

Scarcely enough differentiation. . . The line of
trees against the sky, there. . . I appreciate your
problem, friend. . . only too well . . .

(Again SID's *sole response is the erratic giggle,
slowly building in intensity.)*

Look at me, Sid? Do you think I fill the bill?

(SID *looks round.)*

SID.   *(Nodding his head)* Sure. Why not?

MAN.   I'm not too. . . unlike?

SID.   On the contrary. . . very like. . . I can see him,
stood there, the living image of you. Same height,
same build. . . very similar. . . Colour of hair right. . .
he could easily have got the shoes without me
knowing. . . you might. . . that is. . . *(He giggles)*
yes. . . the very spit. . . as though nothing had
changed, at all . . . except for. . . but for the. . .
(and he looks downcast)

MAN.   Still, we must make do, as best we can. . . And
we'll see how we get on. No?

(And SID *returns to his drawing. The* MAN
watches him for a few moments.)

I'd try a darker blue, if I were. . . you. You don't
mind the odd. . . the occasional suggestion? No. . ?
Good. . . as dark as you can find. . .

SID.   You're right, you know. . . that might do it. . . I
sometimes wish I had oils. . . that I was an oil
painter. . . chalk can be so messy. . . and if there's
one thing I hate it's. . . mess of any kind. . .

(He blows chalk-dust away, and continues to draw.)

Disorder. . . of any kind. . .

(The MAN *has switched his attention to the tray.
He holds it at an angle in front of him, so that the
beans jump and juggle across it.*

SID *concentrates on his drawing. The* MAN *glances
at* SID. SID *still giggles erratically, but pays no
attention to the* MAN.

The MAN *reaches inside his overcoat, and draws*

out a large green muffler. *He wraps it round his
neck, then stands for a moment or two, stroking
it. Then he crosses towards his own pitch, beside
the railings.*

SID *glances up, and sees the muffler. His giggling
chokes, then he gives a series of uncoordinated
jerks. These are accompanied by incoherent half-
animal, half-childlike cries, midway between
sobbing and laughter.*

The MAN *ignores* SID. *Instead, he looks round as
though eager to attract custom, his expression
alert.*

SID's *eyes switch from the muffler to his paintings,
and back again. His spasmodic limb-movements
are still accompanied by the erratic giggling. This
grows louder, more agonising, as:*

The lights slowly dim)

THE END

I DIDN'T ALWAYS LIVE HERE

A Play in Three Acts

I Didn't Always Live Here was first performed in the Glasgow Citizens' Theatre on 18th April 1967, with the following cast:

MARTHA	Irene Sunters
AMIE	Rosamund Burne
ELLEN	Anne Kidd
JACK	James Copeland
WORKMAN	James Gibson
HIS MATE	Angus Macaulay
FRANCIS DUGGAN	Dermot Tuohy
BURLY JIM	Walter Jackson
CHICK	Harry Walker
MacWHURRIE	Roy Boutcher

The play was directed by Michael Meacham.

The present text was first performed by Dundee Repertory Company on 19th June 1973. The part of MARTHA was again played by Irene Sunters. The play was directed by Stephen MacDonald

The play is set in Glasgow and the principal action is set in the present. Flashbacks are:

ACT I:	the 1930's (during the Depression)
ACT II:	the early 1940's (during the Blitz)
ACT III:	the late 1940's (after the War)

ACT I

Lights up on MARTHA's *room. She is in an old rocking-chair, swinging to and fro. Budgie chirping in its cage.*

MARTHA.   What's all your fuss about, son? Stop your
skraiking, I can't make out a thing you're saying.
How do you think I can make out what you're
saying? Without my aid? When my battery's run
down? Fine I know what you want. Not seed,
not cuttlefish. Water. That not right? Don't you
fret. Get your water in good time, so you will.
I'll see to that. Can you not see I'm having a bit
of rest?

Plenty water up there, up there in the attic. Is
that what you're trying to tell me? Don't I
know it. But I've learnt my lesson, so I have. I
learned my lesson the last time. The Fire Brigade
has more to do than go rescuing budgies. That'll
not happen again, not by my way of it. If Jack
was here, mind you, it wouldn't be water you'd
be getting. A drop of Guinness, like as not. That'd
keep you cosy under your feathers. Look, you'd be
as good saving your voice so you would . . .

*(She swings in the chair. Then she tries to rise,
but leans back again.)*

My leg . . . oh, my leg . . . it's no use, son. Just
have to wait your patience, so you will. If I
could only manage across the landing, it'd make
all the difference. But it's no use. No use at all.
And it's days since she's been. Amie. Seems like
weeks. Her and her fancy ways, that pernickety
about so many things. I wonder what she's up to.
Mind you, between you and me, son, it's kind of
peaceful without her . . .

(She chuckles and the budgie chirps as the lights dim.

The lights come up on AMIE's *room: Radio music in the background.* AMIE *is on the telephone.)*

AMIE.   . . . I've been trying to get through for I don't know how long, Donald, it gets worse and worse. No, all I was wondering was when you might manage round, to uplight the books. I thought they might be of use to your fiancée, yes to Gloria. Her being interested in literature, that sort of thing. It'd be lovely to see you again. Yes, I've got them all laid-out and dusted. How's your mother keeping, by the way? Oh, I'm so glad. I'm glad she's got over it so quick. Mind you, it's amazing these days. Oh, much the same as usual. I can't grumble. I said I can't grumble. . . Look, hold on, don't hang up. . .

(She crosses to the radio and turns down the music; then back to the telephone.)

Hello, are you still there? I was afraid you might have rung off. When did you say you could call, you and Gloria? Oh, well, any day except Thursday, that's my sewing-bee. Oh here, I clean forgot to tell you. Sammy. He's away again. I said Sammy's away again. No, it keeps crackling, it must be at both ends. Yes, he just vanished, into the blue. Something must've come over him. I'm near demented, I don't mind telling you, It's a week yesterday. With never a word. I've contacted the Police, they couldn't have been more considerate, but there's been no sign. I haven't been able to sleep a wink. I should never have left him in the house alone. Yes, I'll just keep hoping. Anyway, I mustn't detain you any more, Donald. You've been most sympathetic. Give my love to Gloria. And take care of yourself, bye-bye.

(She replaces the receiver.)

Young folks nowadays. Their sense of considera-tion's *non est*. And sniggering about Sammy. I could hear him. And that damned fiancee of his, not his type at all. Oh, my sprouts, they'll have stuck to the pan . . .

(She exits.

Lights and music down.

Lights up on MARTHA; *the budgie chattering.)*

MARTHA.   Not as if I always lived here, mind you.
Is it son? No, I started off in Govan. Never
dreamt in those days I'd end up this side of the
river. Real step up in the world, that was. When
Jack and me moved across. That was the time he
changed his job, and all. Got into a yard in Partick.
And his first day, while they were brewing up,
some of the others had started arguing, and Jack
had joined in. And they all stopped talking and
looked at him. Till one of them said. 'What are
you interfering for?' And Jack said he wasn't
interfering, he was just venturing an opinion. And
he was telt, 'You're not a Partick man; you're a
Govan man.' They kent it in his voice. That's
what they meant by interfering. Couldn't tell a
thing like that nowadays, could you, son. He
was proud of being a Govan man. But it was a
step up, settling on the other side of the river.
I've been here ever since, and I'm grateful for it.
Despite everything, I'm grateful for it . . .

*(A knock at the door. She stops rocking the chair
and looks up.)*

Aye, who is it?

ELLEN.   *(Off)* It's Ellen. Can I come in?

MARTHA.   The door's off the sneck.

(ELLEN *enters. She is young, attractive.)*

ELLEN.   How are you, Martha?

MARTHA.   So it's yourself. Bit of trouble from the
leg, that's all.

ELLEN.   Have you been eating?

MARTHA.   I haven't been to the Ritz, if that's what
you mean. Too much rich food's bad for the
stomach, my mother used to say. Not that it
was something she was accustomed to.

ELLEN.   There's some things for you. *(She lays down paper bags.)* And some eggs.

MARTHA.   Thanks, lassie. That's kind of you. I can always go an egg.

ELLEN.   Last time I called you'd been having trouble with the roof. Has anyone come about it?

MARTHA.   No, not so far.

ELLEN.   They promised to send someone.

MARTHA.   Give them another couple of days, lass. Since the storm, you know how busy they've been.

ELLEN.   I suppose so. Can I have a look?

MARTHA.   Please yourself.

(ELLEN *goes up to the attic.)*

ELLEN.   Who fitted it out for you?

MARTHA.   It was my man Jack that did it. Oh, a long while back.

ELLEN.   Is that his telescope?

MARTHA.   That's right. Got it at the Barrows.

ELLEN.   Was he an astronomer?

MARTHA.   It was for doing his pools. He was aye one for his coupon, Jack. And one day he came in with the telescope. It was to be his new system. To beat the jackpot. You see, he made all the teams stars. And he worked out the results by the galaxies. He used to work out what teams would be in the ascendant and what ones was in the descendant. You should have seen his plans, and his diagrams.

ELLEN.   The damp is terrible up here. Did he ever win?

MARTHA.   Win? Not him. The Rangers went into eclipse, and that was that. Mind you, he had his fun, the soul. The mug.

ELLEN.   I never know when you're in earnest and when you're pulling my leg. One of these days I'll pull yours.

100

MARTHA. Well, when you do, make sure it's not the
rheumaticky one. That not right, son?

ELLEN. *(Coming down)* When did the doctor last come?

MARTHA. Oh, he gave me some pills. Two boxes.
One for my leg and the other to get me to sleep.
I keep wondering, if I was to take a couple from
each, would it put my leg to sleep.

ELLEN. He must have told you of the danger of the
damp. To your health.

MARTHA. He can't be expected to give me preferential
treatment.

ELLEN. Something will have to be done.

MARTHA. You've not to say a word to the factor.

ELLEN. It's all right. I'm thinking of the Service
Group. I'll see what they can do. I mean, one
downpour, one good night's rain, and that's you.
With the roof in. And the budgie there doing the
backstroke. You said, before, you've nowhere to
go.

MARTHA. Right enough.

ELLEN. Have you enquired . . . about . . . about
going into a home?

MARTHA. You know my feelings about that.

ELLEN. But Martha . . .

MARTHA. *This* is my home, Ellen.

ELLEN. Could I not persuade you at least to put
your name . . .

MARTHA. You'll have to speak up . . . my aid . . .

ELLEN. Won't you put your name down? In case?

MARTHA. My name's going on no list. Anyway,
what about the wee fellow there. They might not
allow budgies. Folk don't seem to care about
animals these days. I had a friend had to pay a
bus fare--for a mouse. And there was another old
woman, when she went they just put her cat to
sleep. You'd have thought they might have
found a home for it, somewhere.

ELLEN. You'd have thought so, Martha.

MARTHA. Still, you can never be too careful about
that sort of thing.

ELLEN. What sort of thing?

MARTHA. Funerals and that. I mind there was an old
body lived near us in Elder Street. This is going
back a bit. And she was aye one for a cheery word.
Agnes Sampson her name was. Do you a good turn
as soon as look at you. And when you said, how
could you pay her back, she used to smile and say,
'Just grace my funeral.' And then, Jack heard that
Agnes Sampson had passed away—and he found
out when the funeral was, and he went. And you
know this, there wasn't a soul he recognised. None
of her cronies, no one. And the next day he met a
couple of her old pals and he said to them, they
might have done the decent thing by her. By Old
Agnes. And they said, what did he mean. And he
said how he'd been at her funeral. And they said
that was queer, for they'd been talking to her that
morning, spry as an old boot. So they jaloused it
must have been another Agnes Sampson. And they
laughed at my Jack and said, 'Did you not make
sure?' And all he could say was, 'I didn't open the
box, if that's what you mean!' That's my leg a bit
better already . . . amazing what a crack does.
You're looking real bonny the day.

ELLEN. Do you not have any relations?

MARTHA. There was some on Jack's side. But we kind
of lost touch. You know how it is.

ELLEN. I know.

MARTHA. Over the years.

ELLEN. Well, here, I was just looking in. I haven't
really time to stay. But I'll be back. And I'll
bring you a new battery for that aid of yours. Is
there anything else you'd like? How about a bag
of coal? Are you sure? Well, as I said, I'll
contact the Service Group. And I'll let you know
the outcome. All right?

MARTHA. There's not much I can do to stop you.
But you'll be—

ELLEN.   There's no need for you to worry. I promise you that. Cheerio meantime, Martha.

MARTHA.   Cheerio. Thanks again.

(ELLEN *exits.*)

MARTHA.   I clean forgot to ask her to fill your saucer, son. Still the leg seems a thing easier. I might be able to manage. If it's loyal enough . . . *(She rises)* A bag of coal? I mind when we could've done with a fistful. . . They were bad times, for us all. Bad enough for me. But Jack, he was a man. I'll never forget yon as long as I live.

(The lights change:

MARTHA *exits.*

The door opens and JACK *enters wearily. Slowly, he unlaces his boots and takes off his jacket. From the pockets he takes lumps of coal and throws them in the grate. Then he lies down.)*

MARTHA.   *(Off)* Is that you, Jack.

JACK.   Aye, it's me.

MARTHA.   *(Off)* How did you get on? Did you get anything?

JACK.   What do you mean, did I get anything?

(Pause.)

A few bits of coal. Lying in Stobcrosse Street. There was some more, but a whole gang of fellows got there first. Had it lifted before it had stopped rolling, if you ask me.

MARTHA.   *(Off)* Nothing else?

JACK.   No. *(He rises, paces the room)*

MARTHA.   *(Off)* Nothing in the way of work, Jack? *(Pause)* Did you try the collier? Jack, did you hear me?

(She enters: a younger MARTHA, *as she appears in all the flashback scenes.)*

JACK.   I've tried him twice. It's no go.

MARTHA.   And the carter?

JACK.   I've tried him and all. Me and ten hundred others.

MARTHA.   Just have to keep at them, is that it?

JACK.   Look, face up to it, will you. I tell you it's no go.

MARTHA.   What happened?

JACK.   What do you mean?

MARTHA.   The carter? What did he say?

JACK.   The same as he said the last time, and the time before and the time before. That he had no jobs, that he had paid off, that there were others before me anyway.

MARTHA.   He didn't need to say that, did he?

JACK.   He had every right. He can say what he likes. He's in a position to. Anything he bloody well likes.

MARTHA.   *(Pause)* Is there nothing else? How did Attie get his job?

JACK.   You mean in the municipal gardens? His sister's man's a Councillor.

MARTHA.   Could you not try, I mean for a job in the gardens? They'll need folk there.

JACK.   Let them need folk. No, I've tried. With all the others. It's no go, Martha. It's almost a relief to have the lad in the hospital this spell, it means one less mouth to feed.

MARTHA.   He'll be out soon.

JACK.   Damn sight too soon.

MARTHA.   *(Pause)* Andy not help? Eh?

JACK.   Andy's too busy feathering his own nest. Lining his own belly.

MARTHA.   When the boy does come back, he'll have to eat, Jack. And what with the cold weather setting in . . .

JACK.   What are you trying to say?

MARTHA. I mean, fuel as well as food. Up till now we've been lucky, but we're soon going to need fuel as well as food.

JACK. *(Comes to stairs)* So? Have I not been up and down as far as the docks? To hell, Martha, you know I have. I've done my best, so I have. But there's others. I mean in the queues, in the lines, in the hunt for fuel. I've got some, if they knew I had it they'd tear the place down to get at it. That's why I brought it in. I've done my best to get fuel, and that's the best I can do.

MARTHA. I don't mean that, Jackie. I don't mean looking for fuel.

JACK. What do you mean, then?

MARTHA. I mean going and asking Andy.

JACK. I've asked Andy.

MARTHA. Could you not bring yourself to ask him again? Could you—for the boy's sake?

JACK. No, I couldn't!

MARTHA. Jackie, why not?

JACK. I'll tell you why not. Because I've got . . .

MARTHA. You've got what?

JACK. I tell you, I've got . . . my pride.

MARTHA. Don't think I don't know that.

JACK. No, you're right, Martha. Not any longer. I haven't any pride left. You can't afford that sort of thing nowadays. I asked him, Martha. Do you believe me, I asked him. Today. But he says it's still no go. He's got nothing.

MARTHA. We'll have to keep hoping, that's all. I'm sorry I riled you, Jack.

JACK. It'll work out all right. You wait and see.

MARTHA. It's got to.

JACK. I'm telling you, it will. It'll be all right, for you and the boy. *(Pause)* To hell with fuel, Martha. You'll have no need of fuel. I'll see

to that. *(As she looks at him)* I'll save up. And
buy you a fur coat. No, I mean it. I'll get all
prepared . . . in my jodphurs and one of them
fancy-wallah bonnets. And I'll go Big Game
hunting. Me and a squad of sherpas. On safari.
In Bellahouston Park. And I'll shoot a great big
shaggy wild bear . . . or maybe an Oliphant . . .
and have it made into a fur coat, for you. How's
about that?

MARTHA.   Oliphants don't have fur.

JACK.   The ones I catch will. And a pair of ear-muffs
for the boy . . . for when he comes out . . .
furry ear-muffs . . . for the wee fella . . .

MARTHA.   I respect you, Jack. Honest to God, I do.
Whatever things come to. You don't know how
much it means to me, that you love him in the
way you do . . . him and me . . .

JACK.   How's about a cup of tea, eh? There's one made.

(JACK *smacks her on the bottom.*
MARTHA *exits.)*

MARTHA.   *(Off)* It's poured, Jack.

(JACK *takes a few more pieces of coal from his
pocket, throws them in the grate. He takes a model
aeroplane from the mantelpiece, exits with it.)*

JACK.   Coming. Zoom!

*(The lights fade.
Lights come up on* AMIE's *room.
The doorbell rings.
AMIE answers eagerly.
It is the* SLATER *and his* MATE.)

AMIE.   *(Her face falls)* Oh.

SLATER.   Were you not expecting us, like?

AMIE.   I thought for a moment . . . it might be Sammy.

SLATER.   Sammy? *(To his* MATE) Who the hell's
Sammy?

(His MATE *shrugs.)*

AMIE.   Who are you?

MATE. Sidney.

SLATER. Slaters.

MATE. Aye, Slaters.

AMIE. Must you . . . Do you have to . . . come in?

SLATER. Well we're no' pitching wur tent oot here.

AMIE. What I mean is—

SLATER. See and wipe your boots, Sid.

MATE. Sidney.

> *(They enter. Both have haversacks. The MATE carries a bag of tools, which he is about to put on the carpet.)*

AMIE. Just a minute . . . I'll get you a newspaper.

SLATER. You're wasting your time, he cannae read.

> *(But she returns with papers. She puts one underneath the bag, and others on the chair the SLATER is about to lower himself into.)*

Right, Sid. Let's get wired in.

MATE. How often do I have to tell you, it's Sidney.

AMIE. Wired into what?

SLATER. Wur piece.

MATE. I don't like being abbreviated.

SLATER. See's my thermos.

> (MATE *hands him his thermos, and starts eating.)*

Chocolate Penguins again!

MATE. Aye. Fancy wan?

SLATER. Wouldnae mind. *(As* MATE *rummages)* Huv you got wan tae spare?

MATE. Sure. *(He munches, hands over a chocolate biscuit which the* SLATER *takes a bite from)* My sister works in Macdonalds. She brings them home every night. . . in her knickers!

(SLATER *chokes.*

Pause.)

AMIE. *(Trying to recover her composure)* I must say, you took your time about coming.

SLATER. Took wur time! We ran all the way. Faster nor a pair of bloody whippets, so we are. Look at him, he's still peching.

AMIE. If I've rung once, I've rung a dozen times.

SLATER. Save your breath, missus, we've heard it all before. *(As she is about to interrupt)* Look, you're not the only wumman in Glasgow that's got a leaky roof. *(Pours tea)* Anyway we was round last week. Naebody in. Tuesday morning.

AMIE. I remember, the bell went. I was having my inhalation. I couldn't risk coming out from under.

MATE. Your inhalation?

SLATER. You're too young.

(They both chew.)

AMIE. May I take the liberty of asking when you intend to start?

SLATER. Soon as we've had wur piece. I mean, don't tell us you grudge us wur wee bite! Sid needs it. Afore he goes up on the roof there. For stamina. Builds him up. He looks like the original seven-stone weakling, doesn't he? Don't you believe it. Deceptive. Once he's had his piece, once he's out there, there's no stopping him. That right, Sid?

MATE. *(Mouth full)* Sidney! ! !

SLATER. See what I mean!

AMIE. I'm going out. And I couldn't possibly leave you here. I'm sorry. In any case, you can't get access via here. It's boarded off.

SLATER. Cannae get . . . What's that? You mean we've come all the way up here for tae tackle a roof we cannae get onto! *(To MATE)* You'd better say Shazam, quick!

AMIE. It's through next door's attic.

SLATER. Across the stair-held?

AMIE. Across the landing, yes.

SLATER. Could you no have telt us, afore we settelt wurselves doon?

AMIE. I wasn't given much opportunity.

SLATER. Nae need tae loss the tottie.

AMIE. I beg pardon?

SLATER. Keep the heid. All right, I can tell when we're no wantit. *(Gathers his things)* Come on. We'll can take a gander at across the way. By that time, it'll be wur lunch break. Open the door for us.

(AMIE *opens the door.*)

AMIE. How long . . . do you expect the job will take?

MATE. How can we tell you that, afore we've seen it?

AMIE. Can't you give me . . . even a rough idea?

SLATER. Couple of year should see us through. With a bit of luck. Unless he goes doon with diphtheria again. *(To his* MATE) I hope you didnae drap ony crumbs . . .

(They exit.
AMIE *shuts the door firmly.*
She puts on the chain.
The lights fade, and come up on MARTHA's *room, as the* SLATER *and his* MATE *reach her door. A knock, and she answers.)*

All right, dearie, it's only us. We've come fur tae have a deck at the roof. *(As he comes in)* See her through there . . . Fair gets her tonsils in a twist, does she no?

MARTHA. I hoped you'd come. It's been . . . getting pretty bad . . . There was a tarpaulin for a while . . . so they said . . . But it must have slipped, or been blown away.

SLATER. Someone nicked it, mair like. Anyway, relax. . . him and me'll have a gander. Up here, is it? *(He goes to the attic)* See the state of this ceiling. Noah's bloody ark! When were you last up here? Hie, see's a length of wood. Tae prop open

109

the skylight. *(As* SIDNEY *is halfway down)*
Sidney!

(SIDNEY *stops.)*

No you! I've remembered. I kent the name remind-
ed me of someone. Rang a bell. I've got it. It was
yon fellow I use tae dae my Powderhall training
with. Sidney the Brick, we cried him. Going back
years, mind.

MARTHA.   Did I hear you say Sidney the Brick?

SLATER.   Aye, what way?

MARTHA.   My man kent him. My man was a sprinter
for a while. Got taken on for the Powderhall. A
couple of fly men took him over for a couple of
years, and that was him in it up to the neck. Never
got him anywhere, mind you, except running up
and down Glasgow Green with a paper bag over his
head. I've heard him talking about Sidney the
Brick.

MATE.   And his wee brother, I suppose they cried him
Sidney the Half brick?

SLATER.   *(To* MARTHA) What was your man's name?

MARTHA.   Went under Jackie Park. We had a single end
in Govan at the time. 1922, near enough. I mind
once, when they were sharing their winnings, Jack
had it all worked out in advance, what every man
was to get. By long division like. But no the Brick.
When Jack said 'so much' the Brick put his hand
on the bag and said, 'oh no, you don't. We're
having none of your fancy dan mathematics. We'll
get this stack of notes changed into two-bob bits,
and we'll go round and round, till they're all done.'

SLATER.   Head case. Did Jackie Park not have a bit of
trouble, one time? And get himself carved up?

MARTHA.   They wanted him to run with weights. But
he wouldn't have it. That was one reason he got
out. Couldn't take that side of it.

SLATER.   Aye, I mind hearing how he ran a bit foul of
Francis Duggan and all. Yon was a hard case, was
he not!

MARTHA. My Jack couldn't stomach the likes of yon. Neither he could.

SLATER. *(To* MATE) Can you get us a bit of wood, to jam this skylight up.

MARTHA. I've a bit in the kitchen.

(She exits to the kitchen.)

MATE. Is that a telescope?

SLATER. What the hell does it look like?

MATE. There's no need to be offensive.

SLATER. Och, away back to your mammy.

MARTHA. Will this do you?

(MARTHA *has brought in a spar of wood.* SID *goes down and collects it from her, then takes it up.)*

SLATER. Thanks a lot. Now, how's about getting some work done? Out you get, and I'll can pass the stuff out to you. You'll have to watch where you put your feet—place is like an abandoned doocot.

MATE. Is it safe?

SLATER. Of course it's safe.

MATE. Doesn't look safe to me.

SLATER. What the hell are you asking for, then? Don't get carried away, that's all. Don't start imagining you're in the press box at Hampden—and leaning over to follow the flight of the ball. Or your mammy would have to start thinking again.

MARTHA. Are you all right up there?

SLATER. Fine, dearie. Here, it's coming back to me now. I heard some funny things about Jackie Park. It was saying Francis Duggan that sparked me off. You know, about the graft and that. It was the same with the dogs. Never the winners that got the money, but the backers. And the tricks they used to get up to. Feeding them a pie or two. Or putting elastic bands round their toes. Same idea as weighted running-boots. To give the wrong impression. You could never have retired to Capri on the proceeds. But that doesn't mean it was to be sniffed at. *(He turns to his* MATE*)* What are you waiting for? Crying out loud, are you no set up yet? *(Calls to* MARTHA*)* We'll deposit wur stuff doon here, and we'll can have wur lunch-break after we've done a rekky ootside. Right?

(But MARTHA *has gone, to the kitchen.)*

(To his MATE*)* Have you no wedged that skylight yet?

MATE. It's . . . this bit of wood.

SLATER. What's up with it?

MATE. It's six inches short, at the wan end.

SLATER. *(Gasps in disbelief, then)* Christ, if all the women in Govan was laid end tae end . . . you wouldnae know where tae begin!

(He wedges the skylight, and they exit to the roof. The lights on the attic fade.

Church bells. A dog whines off: we hear MARTHA *comfort it. Knock at the door. Then another, heavy.*

Pause.
MARTHA *comes from the kitchen: younger, once again.*
She opens the door.
Two men stand there.

MARTHA. It's you.

JIM. Who'd you think it was, King Billy?

MARTHA. What do you want? Who's this?

JIM. This is Mr. Duggan, Martha. We've come for a friendly chat with Jack. The very thing for a Sunday morning.

DUGGAN. Get on with it.

MARTHA. I'm not wanting trouble, Jim, honest to God I'm not. What do you want him for?

DUGGAN. Is he in?

MARTHA. Jack?

JIM. Aye, Jack. Or he'll be at the church, like? Always
a man for the church-going was Jack. Must be one
of those new churches that has new ideas, you
know, appetizers like, for to attract folk to God. A
bar in the vestry, and the old pitch and toss school
in the back yard. That it, eh? Come on, where is
he?

MARTHA. In his bed, where he deserves to be. He's
been on the back shift.

JIM. Didn't know he had a job. What's he do, make
doughnuts?

DUGGAN. We'd like a chat with him.

MARTHA. What about?

JIM. You heard the old story about going to see a man
about a dog? Well, we've *come* to see your man
about a dog.

MARTHA. You've come to the wrong place, Burly Jim.
My man's straight as a die. He'll not go in with any
of your jakes, I'll can tell you. So if you've come
to ask him to follow your footsteps, you might as
well save your breath.

DUGGAN. We have wasted about enough time. Get
him in.

MARTHA. You can't talk to me like this, not in my
own house.

DUGGAN. Whose own house? I know whose house this
is. It's not your Jack's name that's on the title deed,
I'll tell you that for free. Get him in. And look,
you needn't go calling the bogies or any of that
lot, all we want's a friendly chat.

MARTHA. Wait here, will you.

*(She exits towards bedroom. DUGGAN sees a
photograph of a greyhound. He lifts it, shows it to
BURLY JIM. Then they snigger. JACK comes in,
in pyjamas and slippers.)*

JACK. What's the joke, eh?

JIM. Joke, Jack? Aw, we must've missed it.

113

JACK. Well, Duggan?

DUGGAN. Mr. Duggan to you.

JACk. What do you want? *(Pause)* Mister . . . Duggan?

DUGGAN. *(Pause. Holds out photograph)* This yours?

JACK. What, the photograph?

DUGGAN. No, what's on it.

JACK. The dog?

DUGGAN. Aye, what do you think? Well, you haven't answered the question.

JACK. You know it is.

DUGGAN. Oh, we know, do we?

JACK. Of course you know. What's up, Jim?

DUGGAN. How about you helping us out. How's about you telling us what we don't know? How's about that, eh, son?

JACK. Like what?

DUGGAN. Like what happened to that dog last night at the track?

JACK. What happened? What do you mean what happened?

DUGGAN. You explain to him.

JIM. You were at the track last night, eh Jackie? You and your dog here, eh?

JACK. Of course I was. You know that.

DUGGAN. You were there? Our eyes weren't deceiving us? We didn't make a mistake, did we, think some other bloke was you, get it all wrong, eh? Are you sure now, Jackie? Just cut the patter. Your dog was in the salver trot. The straight run. 8.30. Your dog Wee Jeannie was in the 8.30 last night?

JACK. You saw it run.

DUGGAN. That's the point, Jack, it didn't run.

JACK. Of course it ran, to hell, what do you think it was? Do you think there was a switch and all, with some other dog?

114

JIM.   Your dog didn't run.

JACK.   It did.

DUGGAN.   It didn't.

JACK.   It did—

DUGGAN.   Not. It did not run. It bloody well dandered.
It cut a bloody caper and then flaked out. It tripped
over its own belly in the back straight. It did not
'run', son!

JACK.   It didnae win, if that's what you're saying.

JIM.   Did it get examined afterwards?

JACK.   Course it got examined afterwards.

DUGGAN.   Examined? Should have X-rayed it, might
have found a couple of pies in its gut. Eh, Jack?
What have you to say to that one?

JACK.   You're talking rubbish, Duggan . . .

DUGGAN.   *(Pause)* What?

JACK.   I mean you've made some mistake, like. It's
easy done, I mean, the race wasn't fixed or anything,
but these things just happen, I mean Wee Jeannie
here, she was maybe expected to win, but —

DUGGAN.   She was backed to romp it.

JIM.   We had her backed stiff, mate.

DUGGAN.   That dog was to win. To come in first. To
skelp the lot. That was arranged. That was how it
was to be. And my friend here and me, we had put
the lot on, week's wages, the lot. And your
mucking dog fouled up and didn't come in.

JACK.   You can't prove that and you know it. I had
nothing to do with it.

DUGGAN.   Tell me one thing, did you have a bet on?
On the big dog?

JIM.   Bet he had a wad on. Back-shift and all.

DUGGAN.   Belt up. Well, Jack? How about Wee Jeannie?
Was it fed a couple of pies or was it? You can
always tell by performance, never mind what's
said beforehand, always the performance that

115

counts. What did you have on the other dog—the big one that came in, eh?

JACK.   Not a nickel.

JIM.   That's not what we got from—

JACK.   Look, I've done my sprinting at Powderhall. I've had them all at me. They've tried to use me, but I was never used. No one ever used me. To fix a race or to weight my shoes or any of yon. Yon was for the second-graders, the mugs. And I tell you honest to God and hope to be struck dead it was never my fancy. And the same applies with Wee Jeannie. Wee Jeannie didn't come in, well, that's up to her. No one fed her anything, no one fixed her, she just didn't go so good that day. She's an unreliable animal, I know that, Bert knows that, anyone that wants to back her ought to know that. She's a temperamental dog. You get temperamental dogs. Dogs is highly-strung. Like, well like racehourses. Just the same. Wee Jeannie, see she's highly strung . . .

JIM.   Bloody well ought to be.

JACK.   Might do badly one night out, come in the next. There's no telling what'll happen.

DUGGAN.   Except you'll get a wad of notes in your hand at the tail-end of the meeting. That'll be to keep her in special dog-biscuits, seeing as what she's temperamental, I'll suppose?

JACK.   I've told you all I can tell you. There's nothing else. If you think she'd been fed before the race, you don't want to come to me, you want to go to the track, or you want to ask Bert. That's what to do, you go and ask Bert. He'll tell you the same as I've told you.

DUGGAN.   So we'll go and ask Bert. Where do you keep the dog?

JACK.   At home. Lovely dog, she is. Honest, I wouldn't do a thing like what you've been describing. I couldn't afford it, I mean to say, do you think I'd bugger you up, and then stick around knowing you was on the spot to carve me up any time you wanted?

116

JIM. So your boy doesn't plunk the school to get special soaking meal for Wee Jeannie?

DUGGAN. It looks like we made a big mistake, Jack.

JACK. It does, Mister Duggan. I'm glad you see it that way.

DUGGAN. Francis is the name, Jackie. Have a cigar.

JACK. Thanks, Francis, but I don't smoke them.

DUGGAN. How about giving it to the dog, eh?

JIM. Aye, give it to Wee Jeannie, how's about that?

DUGGAN. Well, our apologies, we've no alternative but to accept your no for an answer. You see how it was, our money all gone down the drain, and your dog had been the form dog. Dead cert, eh Jim?

JIM. Aye, dead cert right enough. *(He laughs)*

DUGGAN. But there we are. Mustn't jump to hasty conclusions. Have to accept your no for an answer, Jackie.

JACKIE. But you do believe me?

DUGGAN. *(Slaps him on the back)* Course we do. Course we believe you. Don't we not, Jim?

JIM. Aye, sure.

DUGGAN. Well . . .

JACK. You not want to say goodbye to the wife? She was, well she's a thing jumpy these days, what with the work and that, and she thought, well, she was a bit feared when you came in, so I think she'd want to say cheerio to you, like. I'll give her a shout through.

DUGGAN. Nice idea. Wouldn't want to go without saying goodbye to her.

JACK. *(Calls)* Martha, Martha pet.

MARTHA. *(Off)* Yes, Jackie. What is it? *(She enters)* What's up? Is everything all right?

JIM. Course everything's all right, Martha. Just going.

117

There'd been a wee, well mistake.

JACK. They thought, Jim and Francis thought, it was all a put-up job at the stadium last night.

MARTHA. That's silly, my man's not the kind—

DUGGAN. We know that. It was all a mistake. We'd got a hold of the wrong end of the stick, that's all. Got a bit hot under the collar, that was it. Where's Wee Jeannie anyway? Where do you keep her?

MARTHA. *(Gesturing)* Through in the kitchen.

JACK. Do you want to see her before you go? That'll convince you she's all right. You'll take to her.

JIM. No, we'd better be getting on our way. There's the Army on the march. If we're not quick, we'll maybe get converted.

DUGGAN. Och, let's have a gander at the dog while we're here. Aye, you lead on, Jackie boy, let's see the hot favourite, I'll see if I can forgive her for last night.

JACK. Och, you will when you see her. A bonnie dog, a bonnie, bonnie dog. Come on through.

(JACK *leads the two men off.* MARTHA *is left alone.*

Sound of Salvation Army Band, Off but approaching.

We hear murmurs, off, from JACK *and the men.* MARTHA *stands, eyes closed, beating time softly to the music.*

Then, laughter from the men, off: and she looks up.

Pause, and then the men approach, laughing.

JIM. That's a good one, Francis, haven't heard one like that for donkeys. My mate'll split his seams laughing at that the morn. Damn near fall off his crane he will. I'll can help him on his way!

DUGGAN. It's a bonnie dog right enough.

MARTHA. He's real proud of it, so he is. He'd do anything, give anything for it. Go without his meat, ask me. So he would.

DUGGAN. It's a bonnie dog, right enough. I'm sure it'll not let us down again. Come on, but.

JIM. Aye, see you Jackie.

JACK. See you.

DUGGAN. You'll can get back to your bed now. Back to the old pit for the rest of the Sabbath. See you anyway. Oh, how that brings it all back, eh, Jim my boy?

Come on, well.

JIM. See you.

JACK. Aye, sure.

(DUGGAN *and* BURLY JIM *exit.* MARTHA *and* JACK *look at one another. Then* MARTHA *shrugs.* JACK *sits.*

MARTHA *crosses again to window, looks out. She finds her purse, opens it, takes out a coin.)*

JACK. Wonder what they were really after.

MARTHA. Bit of excitement, shouldn't surprise me. Beats me why they go around doing that sort of thing. Put the fear of death into ordinary decent folk. Wee Jeannie wasn't fishy yesterday, was she?

JACK. She's a good dog.

MARTHA. That's not an answer to the question.

JACK. Do I need to answer your question, Martha?

MARTHA. *(Pause, then:)* No, Jack. You don't need to.

(The music has stopped.)

JACK. We've got to eat, Martha.

MARTHA. You will be careful, Jack? What if they kent you had a bet on yon other dog? The dog that won?

JACK. Nothing much they could have done. Might have tried to take it off me, that's about the lot. But not them, just a couple of bags of hot air, them two.

119

At least Burly Jim. Don't fancy the likes of that
Francis Duggan though. Stoop to anything.

MARTHA.   Well, it's over now. At least it got you up!
What are you going to do now?

JACK.   Feed Wee Jeannie and then take her for a run.
Along the river, like as not.

MARTHA.   I'll come with you as far as Mabel's. I've a
couple of blankets to get back off her.

JACK.   Right you are.

> *(Pause.*
> MARTHA *exits.*
> *Suddenly, a scream, off:* JACK *is rooted to the*
> *spot.)*

JACK.   Christ, Martha . . . What is it?

MARTHA.   *(Off)* It's Wee Jeannie. She's foaming at the
mouth.

> (JACK *rushes to the kitchen.)*

JACK.   *(Off)* The Swine. Hold her for me.

MARTHA.   *(Off)* What is it, Jack? What's the matter
with her?

> (JACK *enters.)*

JACK.   That Duggan when he was in, seeing Wee Jeannie,
he gave her a sweetie, and I never thought nothing
of it—where's that bottle?

> (JACK *rushes to the sideboard, opens it, rummages.)*

> The bloody swine . . . *(He searches frantically.*
> *Eventually finds the bottle he is looking for.)*

MARTHA.   *(Off)* Jack, you'll have to hurry . . . Hurry . . .

> *(The Salvation Army Band has started to play*
> *once more: a hymn-tune, close.* JACK *fumbles*
> *with the bottle, opens it, sniffs to make sure it is*
> *the right one, empties some pills into his hand.)*

JACK.   *(Calls)* Get some water . . . In a saucer . . . And
some salt . . . *(He heads for the door.)* It wisnae the
dog's fault . . . They didn't have to go and poison
her . . .

(JACK *exits.*
The lights change.
MARTHA *is back in her rocking-chair. The toy
aeroplane in her hands. The Salvation Army Band
plays jauntily.)*

END OF ACT ONE

MARTHA's *room:* MARTHA *and* ELLEN. ELLEN *is
closing the budgie's cage carefully.* MARTHA *watches
her.*

MARTHA. Thanks, lass. It's not that I can't manage,
it's just that every now and then I find it a bit
difficult. When the saucer starts shoogling. But
that'll do him for the time being. That not right,
son? You can splash about in that to your heart's
content. Right, sit yourself down.

ELLEN. Thanks.

MARTHA. Well, out with it. What are you going to do
with me?

ELLEN. For you.

MARTHA. The same thing, at my age.

ELLEN. Three members of the Service Group are away
this week. So it'll have to wait. I'm sorry about
that.

MARTHA. It can't be helped. Anyway, it's not your
fault.

ELLEN. We ought to be covered, for an emergency like
this. Martha, I can see no alternative but to have a
word with the landlord.

MARTHA. The landlord? I forbid it.

ELLEN. But why?

MARTHA. Easy seen you're not long at this job. He'd
put me out. As soon as look at me. He's got the
power. The law's still on his side.

ELLEN. Not really.

MARTHA. You try and get round it.

ELLEN. I'll have to speak to him, sooner or later. Oh,
before I forget, your new battery. I'll leave it on
the sideboard.

MARTHA. I've done all that can be done. I've spoken
to the rent man. The man that comes with the rent,
I've told him.

ELLEN. What did he say?

MARTHA. Always the same. That the building's due for demolition. It's to come down. For the Ring Road. But I'll have to wait, like everyone else. Even the Slaters, when they did come, said it was scarcely worth doing anything. Other than a patch job.

ELLEN. So you said.

MARTHA. You know what it minds me of? The time Jack came back from the dentist, and he said 'The teeth are all right, but the gums'll have to come out'.

ELLEN. It's a disgrace, so it is. And I'm going to do something about it. I'm going to see him.

MARTHA. Not the landlord, Ellen. I've told you—

ELLEN. The factor, then.

MARTHA. He'll just pass it on.

ELLEN. What if he does?

MARTHA. They can do terrible things to you. You don't realise . . . I knew one woman, she complained to the Rent Tribunal. And they kindled a fire on her stair. Tried to smoke her out. Another time . . . alongside the river . . . they put dog's dirt through an old body's letter-box. Ellen, I couldn't stand the likes of yon . . . Please . . .

ELLEN. I won't mention you by name. I'll make clear I'm acting on my own initiative. Off my own bat. So that nothing rebounds on you.

MARTHA. They'll find out. And you know how they react to Authority.

ELLEN. I'm not Authority. That's what makes me so angry. If only I was, they might listen. But I'm not. I'm not even official. I'm only a community volunteer. I'd be able to do more, if I was in television. If we could get shots taken of your roof, and shown them on television, people would see what conditions were like. It might bring it home to them.

MARTHA. Aye, that might raise a stink, right enough.

ELLEN. The biggest stink wouldn't be raised by folk
wanting to *do* something about it. But by the Lord
Provost and his cocktail councillors—them that
aren't on jaunts to Miami—complaining it wasn't
an accurate picture of the city. There's no slums in
Glasgow. The same as there's never been any gangs.
Because they've persisted in turning a blind eye to
them.They ignore them and hope they'll go away.
It was like that yesterday, it's like that today, and
God help us it'll be like that tomorrow.

MARTHA. Take is easy, lass. Don't get so steamed up
about it.

ELLEN. It makes me sick. *(Pause)* I'm sorry. I'd better
be going. I didn't mean to upset you.

MARTHA. You haven't upset me, don't worry.

> *(As* ELLEN *prepares to leave.)*

There's one thing . . . If your Service Group *does*
come, make sure they wear their tin hats. In case it
starts raining plaster!

> (ELLEN *has reached the door.* MARTHA *shows
> her out, stands there, looks up, then sits as the
> lights change.*
>
> *The attic:* JACK *with his friend* CHICK. *Both in
> Home Guard uniform.*
>
> JACK *polishes telescope.* CHICK *throws darts.*
>
> *Buckets of sand and water.* CHICK *peers through
> the telescope.)*

CHICK. Could you not move that ruddy telescope to
one side?

JACK. I could not.

CHICK. You want to watch it, Jack. There's some folk
might be suspicious, if they was to see a telescope
rigged up, through a tenement roof. I mean, they'd
think you were fraternising, no firewatching.

JACK. Frater-what!

CHICK. I mean with the Germans. How many tenements is there about here, or in Maryhill for that

matter, that have telescopes sticking out through their skylight?

JACK.   There could be hundreds. For all you know. Couldn't there? What's biting you?

CHICK.   I wouldn't say too much about it, that's all. Careless talk costs lives, Jack.

JACK.   Well? So what?

CHICK.   They could say it was . . . a means of communicating with the Axis . . . Of collaborating, like . . .

JACK.   Are you serious? Cos if I thought you were . . .

CHICK.   Take it easy. I'm thinking of you. I mean, you try and convince them.

JACK.   Them?

CHICK.   Try telling them what it's for. See if they believe you.

JACK.   I've told you. It's for keeping an eye on the Park. Someone has to man the defences. When we've won this bloody war, Chick, there's going to be games again. Real games. None of your utility internationals. And they'll need the Park. So I'm here, doing my bit for the Nation. All rigged out, for to preserve the turf. And all you do is scoff. And say I'm . . . fraternising, or something. I'm telling you Chick, if their bombers come across here and start dropping their shit on Ibrox . . . I'll blow them out the sky with my bare hands. I'm telling you, I'll let them have it.

CHICK.   Let's see the colour of your money.

JACK.   Don't let Martha hear you saying that.

MARTHA.   (*Calls*) Would you like a cup of tea, you two?

CHICK.   *(Calls)* Wouldn't mind, Martha.

(JACK *comes down, takes a tray, goes back up.*)

JACK.   Okay . . .

CHICK.   *(Calls)* Thanks, Martha.

(MARTHA *exits.* CHICK *is at the telescope.* JACK *pours the tea.*)

Anyway . . . you can't see Ibrox from here.

JACK.   You what!

CHICK.   In the black-out.

JACK.   I'm trained on it. All worked out by deduction.
By the stars.

CHICK.   How do you know they're on our side?

JACK.   Look Chick, do you not understand? You have
to have something. Don't go mocking. Martha and
me have to have something. To cling to. My boy . . .
Martha and me's boy . . . he's out in Burma. The
least I can do is . . . well, do something that helps
me to keep him in mind. Och to hell, I can't spell
it out for you. I'm past fighting for my country.
That doesn't mean I—can't do something.

CHICK.   Sure. You've done your bit.

JACK.   So it doesn't matter if I get my lot or if I don't.
Fair enough. But until I do, I'm sticking it out. In
the one place I can be near my boy. See this . . . I
wish this was a gun . . . a ruddy great gun, Chick.
Not a footery wee bit of metal with a magnifying
glass in it. But something big . . . I'd bring them
down, so I would. Boom, boom, boom . . . one
after another.

CHICK.   Steady on . . .

JACK.   And anyway, I couldn't. I haven't the reflexes
any more. And I don't know that I'd want to,
when it came to the bit. Wars is all right, if there
was only the one side to think about. The first
time I heard a Gerry pray, in the front line, it
stopped me in my tracks, I can tell you. It made
me see things different. Why should my God be
any better than his? Even if I was to have one? No,
wars is all right, when the bands is playing and the
flags flying. But that isn't war. Not really war. To
blazes, I'm frozen stiff. Come on, and I'll tan the
backside off you. And be careful where you throw
them, or Martha'll think it's raining plaster . . .

CHICK.   Come on, middle for diddle. 301 up.

(The lights dim. Up on AMIE's *room. She sits, with a newspaper.)*

AMIE.   I must put a message in, about Sammy. An appeal. 'Houses to let', that's no use . . . 'Public Notices'? Not really . . . I know, I'll try the Personal Column. He always used to seem so happy, I can't understand. Unless he's been kidnapped. By some Chinese restaurant. Oh, I couldn't bear it . . . What are their rates? Let's see. 30p? 30p a line! Not much scope for descriptive details, I must say. For goodness sake . . . 30p a line . . . that comes to . . . That's ridiculous. I think perhaps I'll leave it . . . Another few days won't make much odds.

(The doorbell rings. She answers, ushers in MR MacWHURRIE. *He has brought flowers, fruit.)*

How lovely to see you, Mr MacWhurrie. Will you have a cup of tea?

MacWHURRIE.   Amie, I'm offered so many cups of tea, on my parish rounds, that—

AMIE.   So you always say. But you'll take one all the same, won't you? Such lovely flowers. They'll be from the Thanksgiving. Tulips were always my sister's favourite, before she emigrated. I'll likely be going out there for a couple of months. After I've got my move over, that is.

MacWHURRIE.   *(As she takes his coat)* Yes, yes . . . of course . . .

AMIE.   It's good of you to remember me. Of the congregation. That's one of the things I miss here . . . my own garden. We always had a garden when we were children. Before father died, of course. Then everything changed. Oh, I must put them into water, straight away.

MacWHURRIE.   Yes, well actually . . . there are two bunches there . . .

AMIE.   So I see. That's extremely generous, Mr MacWhurrie.

MacWHURRIE.   No, you don't understand—

AMIE.   Oh, and only one of them's for me . . . is that it?

127

That's what I thought. Which one's my bunch, Mr MacWhurrie?

MacWHURRIE. Well, I'd thought . . . I hadn't made up my mind, to tell you the truth. That is, perhaps, if you would like to choose . . . indeed, that was what I'd intended.

AMIE. Really? Well, it's so difficult . . . they're both absolutely lovely. Aren't they? Eenie-meenie, miney . . . that one, if I may. Thank you. *(She takes the more attractive bunch)* You're really sure it's all right, me choosing like that? The other bunch will be for . . .

MacWHURRIE. Yes.

AMIE. You haven't been to see her, yet?

MacWHURRIE. Not yet.

AMIE. I do feel honoured. Would you not rather she had . . . no, they're both so lovely. And the perfume . . .

(She goes to the kitchen. He removes his bicycle clips, pockets them, passes a hand wearily across his forehead. She returns, with tea-things.)

I do love flowers, all growing things. You understand, I didn't always live here, Mr MacWhurrie. For a while we lived out of Glasgow, my mother and myself. Out of the soot and grime. But changes come to us all, as you might say. I remember the country, and well, everything, so vividly. Of course I'm just here temporary. You know what temporary means these days mind you. Can't depend on a soul in those offices. Rebates or anything. I've been made a number of offers, but none of them materialised. I mean, you can't just take anything— or anywhere. But with a bit of luck I'll have my new flat one of these days. That's why I've been on to my nephew Donald to come and collect these books. Do you think there might be any you'd like, Mr MacWhurrie?

MacWHURRIE. Does that mean that you anticipate leaving the parish, then?

AMIE. I don't think so. Oh no, I wouldn't want to do that.

128

MacWHURRIE. Ah, I'd wondered if that was what you
wanted to see me about.

AMIE. No, it's about my will, you see, Mr MacWhurrie.
And the change in my plans, owing to Sammy. You
see, I'd always wanted Sammy to have a nice home
when I went. And in my will I had left him well
provided for. Within my means, that is. I was going
to leave a little to the cat and dog home. But with
a provision that it was for the cat side of it. Well,,
anyway, when Sammy went—I'm sure he was
lifted, but that's another story—oh, I didn't think
I'd get over it, Mr MacWhurrie—neither I did—well,
anyway, I thought to myself, I had a long ponder,
and I thought to myself, why leave it till then. You
see, I've a little in shares, some I can't touch but
there is a little. And I thought, specially if I was to
be moving from this district, in gratitude to you,
I'd like to leave a little to the church. A modest
sum. But towards something. I couldn't manage a
whole window, anything on that scale. But I could
contribute. Amie, I said to myself, you could contribute. And so you could, I replied. Another
biscuit?

MacWHURRIE. Have you any idea . . . well, what sum
is involved?

AMIE. The church has been good to me, especially you,
Mr MacWhurrie. Oh, I couldn't say. But I hope,
when it comes, that is, it'll be a nice little nest-egg.

MacWHURRIE. And had you decided, well, what form
it's to take?

AMIE. It's to go towards the new carillon. The carillon
of bells.

MacWHURRIE. I see, Amie.

AMIE. Is that all right?

MacWHURRIE. Yes . . . It's just . . .

AMIE. Just towards it. I mean, they must be terribly
dear. I hope you will accept.

MacWHURRIE. This is extremely gracious of you,
Amie. Don't worry about the size of the contribution, after all, the widow's mite, eh? No, all I was

129

thinking was whether you wouldn't wish to make your contribution perhaps, well, more practical?

AMIE. You're not in favour of the bells?

MacWHURRIE. Please don't mistake me, Amie . . . I am, indeed I am . . .

AMIE. Well, that's that. I just wanted to mention it to you before my removal comes along.

MacWHURRIE. This is most kind, believe you me.

AMIE. I hoped you might see it that way. I mean, I know a lot of folk don't go in for the idea of new bells. The carillon. But I think it's a lovely idea. Lovely. And I wanted to do this, well, out of respect and appreciation for yourself, Mr MacWhurrie. The last man never gave, well, personal attention in the way you do.

MacWHURRIE. It's kind of you to say so. Well, Amie. . . I've several more visits to get in before I go home. And I've a meeting this evening.

AMIE. Meetings, meetings.

MacWHURRIE. This one is about the carillon, I believe.

AMIE. To discuss plans?

MacWHURRIE. There are one or two objections, and these will have to be discussed. And there had been a suggestion that the bequest should be spent in some other way. You see, some folk wonder what practical use a carillon is, and want to get the conditions of the bequest changed, so that the money can be spent on something else.

AMIE. What else could the money be spent on?

MacWHURRIE. Fabric, I suppose. There's dry rot in the organ gallery, and maybe in the steeple. And the hall could do with redecorating.

AMIE. I know, but och, these are all run-of-the-mill things, not what you want to waste a special gift like this on. I mean, I wouldn't want my gift just to be squandered on other well, let's face it, bread-and-butter things. If I thought there was any chance of

130

that I'd take it back straight away.

MacWHURRIE.   I understand.

AMIE.   I knew you would. You're so understanding,
and so sympathetic. You always see the reasons
for people doing things. Could you not manage
another biscuit?

MacWHURRIE.   Really, no. I've overstayed my welcome
as it is.

AMIE.   Oh, you could never do that here, Mr MacWhurrie.
Never. You will still be able to come and visit me,
when I've moved, won't you? I'll still stay a
member of the parish. I ought to be at this end of
the new flats, so it won't be too far. I mean, you'll
have a car by then. You haven't got one yet, have
you?

MacWHURRIE.   No, I still use the bike. Good for the
muscles.

AMIE.   Yes.

MacWHURRIE.   Well, I must be off this time. Thanks
for the cup of tea, Amie. Oh, and thank you for
your generosity.

AMIE.   Oh, it's nothing, really it isn't. I wish I had been
someone like Miss Cameron, and I could have been
the person that donated the lump sum for the
carillon. I'd have loved to do that.

MacWHURRIE.   I'm sure you would, Amie. I'm sure
you would. Well, good-bye. And renewed thanks to
you.

AMIE.   Au revoir, Mr MacWhurrie. Oh, your brief-case,
you don't want to forget that.

MacWHURRIE.   No indeed. Thanks very much. Good-bye,
I mean au revoir.

*(She shows him out. The lights dim. Simultaneously:
the lights rise on* MARTHA's *room. Knock on door.
She answers,* MacWHURRIE *comes in, with
flowers.)*

MARTHA.   Come on in, Reverend, and sit yourself down.
You're later than I'd expected. What lovely
flowers.

131

MacWHURRIE. I'll put them in water for you. Later?

MARTHA. You don't usually spend that long through the wall. I heard you coming up the close.

MacWHURRIE. It wouldn't surprise me if you know what we were talking about, Martha!

MARTHA. Aye, she'd be on about her bells, I suppose.

MacWHURRIE. How do you know about her bells?

MARTHA. You can't stay in a place the likes of this and not know all that's going on in folk's minds. Things just seep through the stonework so they do. A baby wets it nappies in a top flat, it's a burst pipe by the time it reaches the ground floor. Not that you'll find any babies up here, Reverend.

MacWHURRIE. What . . . what do you know about the bells, I wonder?

MARTHA. Nothing much, just the gist. She must've mentioned it to somebody. About wanting to make a donation of some kind. Does that mean she's got money?

MacWHURRIE. She may have a little. But it isn't money she can touch just now.

MARTHA. I see. Anyway, it's none of my business. All I was doing was teasing you. I'm not fishing for information.

MacWHURRIE. What do you think of the idea? Just between you and me?

MARTHA. It's not my place to venture an opinion. But I'm sure some folks could dream up better ways of throwing away their capital. I'd be careful if I was you. She might have her ear to the keyhole.

MacWHURRIE. My fault, I'd no right to draw you. But you took me by surprise, despite what I'd said. But I'm not here to chat about Amie. What about yourself, eh? How have you been, this weather?

MARTHA. Can't grumble.

(Pause.)

MacWHURRIE. It still smells of damp, in the kitchen.

That'll do your rheumatics no good.

MARTHA. You're right. But yon lassie from the Community was here. She says she'll get the, what was it, the Service Group to come and plaster up the ceiling if nothing else.

MacWHURRIE. We can but hope it doesn't rain between now and the Service Group coming.

MARTHA. Do you think it makes any odds? Who ever heard of it giving up raining, because some poor body's roof's caving in? That's not the way rain works, you know as well as I do. That's another thing God hasn't figured out.

MacWHURRIE. Don't talk that way, please. The gift of life is a—

MARTHA. Gift? Who asked for it?

MacWHURRIE. Is a rare gift.

MARTHA. So rare there's 60 million folk has it. Look at China. What's so rare about yon? India?

MacWHURRIE. You know what I meant.

MARTHA. I'm sorry. You shame me, so you do. It's just that I feel I've had about enough, sometimes. Do you ever get that feeling?

MacWHURRIE. Often. All you can do is put your trust in—

MARTHA. Two years, was it they said? They'd have a bed in two years? I'll have a clean white sheet of my own, by then. It's easy to say what to put your trust in. It's not so easy to do it.

MacWHURRIE. That's where faith comes in.

MARTHA. Don't be childish.

MacWHURRIE. Martha . . .

MARTHA. I didn't mean that. I didn't mean . . . anything personal, Reverend. But I have to get it off my chest, now and again.

MacWHURRIE. If that makes it easier for you—

MARTHA. When I think back. . .

133

MacWHURRIE. Well?

MARTHA. I was sitting here, when the news came.
There was my man, my man Jack . . . Some things
make it difficult. Losing your man makes it
difficult. What do you know of that? Of an empty
bed, after years and years? What answers have you
for that?

MacWHURRIE. Get it out of your system.

MARTHA. Out of my system? It is my system. It
comes bursting back, every once in a while, even
at this date, welling up inside me. It's all been so. . .
meaningless.

MacWHURRIE. I'll grant you many things, but not
that. Not that there's no meaning.

MARTHA. It's fine for you. You're the one that has
the yardstick.

MacWHURRIE. Bleak maybe, but not meaningless. I
would deny that.

MARTHA. Deny it, then. What do you know about it?
I went through it. Jack, he went through it. What
was there in the likes of yon? What meaning? Can
you answer me that? From your chapter and
verse.

MacWHURRIE. Martha. . .

MARTHA. He'll know the answer now, so he will, bless
him. If there's any answer to be had. Och, what
does it matter? What does anything matter any
more?

MacWHURRIE. You mustn't say things like that. I
know it's hard. But—

MARTHA. Hard? Of course it's hard. Life's hard. Don't
get me wrong. I'm not moaning, Reverend. I've
been a lucky woman, in lots of ways. Me and Jack
moving here. It was some move for him and all.
One trip on the Govan Ferry, he thought he was
emigrating. Jack done well for me. He didn't
deserve what came to him.

MacWHURRIE. We all feel that, at some time or other.
Especially when a loved one's involved. But I do

believe there's a reason behind it all, even if it isn't
clear to us. There's so much suffering in the world.
Do you not trust in God, Martha?

MARTHA. I'm learning to get on without him.

MacWHURRIE. But you . . . admit there must be some
purpose? Behind things? Otherwise—

MARTHA. When I want one of your sermons, I'll come
to the kirk for it.

MacWHURRIE. You'll be very welcome.

MARTHA. You've a couple of sturdy elders handy,
have you, to carry me there?

MacWHURRIE. I think we could manage even that.

MARTHA. It isn't you I'm getting at, you're not to
think that.

MacWHURRIE. *(Picking up a crochet table-mat)* Did
you make that?

MARTHA. No, my man Jack did. Hands like a navvy,
yet he could do crochet lovelier than any woman.
He used to show regular, at guilds and that.

MacWHURRIE. It's a delicate piece of work.

MARTHA. Your wife would like it, wouldn't she. I'd
like you to take it to her.

MacWHURRIE. I couldn't possibly . . . no, Martha . . .

MARTHA. A woman can aye do with a table-mat.
Anyway, you'll take what's offered you. See here,
I'll put some paper round it. It's all right, I can
manage fine, thanks. *(Rising, she finds a sheet of
paper and wraps the mat)* Now, no arguing. I'd . . .
I'd like her to have it.

MacWHURRIE. My wife will treasure that gift, Martha.

MARTHA. Och, away with you. Watch it doesn't fall
out your pocket on the way home. I hope no-one's
let down your tyres this time.

MacWHURRIE. At the Presbytery meeting next week
I'll raise the matter of—

MARTHA. I'll take what comes to me, without fear or

135

favour. I'm as safe as houses. And the Service Group'll be round any day.

MacWHURRIE.   I'll be back soon.

MARTHA.   Just chap on the door. I'm not likely to be away my holidays.

MacWHURRIE.   And we'll see what we can do.

MARTHA.   Who's the 'we'? You and the good Lord?

MacWHURRIE.   It could be, Martha, it could be. *(Taps the brief-case, into which he has put the tray-cloth)* Thanks once more. I hope there's a meaning behind it all. Or else my life in the ministry's totally wasted. Being a minister doesn't mean I don't have doubts too, you know. It's never easy. All we can do is have faith, Martha. Have faith . . .

(Pause, then he exits. Slowly she closes the door behind him. She leans against it.)

MARTHA.   Aye, faith . . . What was it Jack said about faith? 'Mind and ask at the greengrocer's for a couple of ounces, next time you're out your messages . . .'

(She crosses to the rocking-chair, and sits: as the lights dim. The lights come up on the attic; JACK and CHICK, on home guard duty.)

CHICK.   What's in the boxes, Jack?

JACK.   Groceries.

CHICK.   What the hell for? Are you laying in a siege or something?

JACK.   Save me going up and down the stairs every time I get hungry. Look, when these raids start they're going to be something, Chick. They're not going to call a halt while I go down and put on a tin of soup for myself.

CHICK.   You're off the nut. What are you doing?

JACK.   I'm checking them. Never know who's going to diddle you, in war-time. Fly men making a mint all over the place, short-changing you in the rush.

CHICK.   Have you never opened your bottle? How's

136

about that for abstemious?

JACK. That bottle's not for opening, how often do I
have to tell you? It's being saved, for the day my
boy comes home from the Far East, from Burma.

CHICK. There you are again, giving away military
secrets. What if I was an enemy agent? We're not
supposed to know where the troops are. You spill
the beans, and next minute the news is scooting
across Europe to old Adolf's head-quarters, and
the Gerries change their whole plan of campaign.

JACK. It'll not be the Gerries in Burma, Chick.

CHICK. Makes it worse.

JACK. And my boy's out there. So no funny remarks.
He means a hell of a lot to Martha and me, the boy
does. We want him home safe, when this is tied up.
I've told you, it's what keeps me going. *(Pause)*
Hey, you hear about the English soldiers, up at
Maryhill Barracks?

CHICK. What about them?

JACK. Thought you might have heard. These dozen
English blokes gets posted to the HLI at the
Barracks. And they get there, must've been
Friday night. And they're told, CO's parade, first
thing in the morning. So they get weaving. But
they've never worn the kilt before. So one English
fellow goes up to a Jock and he says, all serious-
like. 'I say, how do you wear your kilt?' And the
Jock says 'Down to there, and you don't wear
anything under it.' And the Englishman says, 'But
how do you keep it up?' So the Jock says 'Braces—
same as trousers.'

CHICK. Bloody Sassenachs!

JACK. So next morning, out on the square, there's the
platoon lined up for inspection. And these
English, they look like they'd slept in their uni-
forms. Scruff. So the officer goes up to one of
them, and prods him with his baton. And
discovers the braces. So he does his nut, and gets a
corporal to open all the men's tunics, and all those
with braces, they cut them. And all the English-
men's kilts fell round their ankles. And underneath

137

they're all bollock-naked. And a crowd got up, in the street. All the womenfolk, all the Maryhill hairies, laughing and cherring. . . You'd never've thought there was a war on.

CHICK. Mind you, they're a hard bunch, the HLI. Black Watch and all. I wouldn't like to be around when old Adolf gets his. *(He makes an imaginary bayonet-thrust.)*

JACK. Think he will?

CHICK. Sooner the better. Can't last for ever. I mean, we're well defended. We've got—well there's you and me for a kick-off. No, his days are numbered.

(JACK polishes the telescope with a rag, in time to the tune.)

(Sings, to "Colonel Bogey")
"Hitler has only got . . . one ball . . ."

Here, you got a can-opener?

JACK. What for?

CHICK. You'd be in some fix with all those tins and no opener, that's all. Got your candles in case the electricity goes off?

JACK. Do you mind Willie MacCandless's boy, Chick? The wee fellow, him that was in the pits for a couple of years. Had a trial for the Jags once. Looked about two stone, with his boots on.

CHICK. What about him?

JACK. He got the VC. In France. It's not confirmed yet.

CHICK. Is the boy alive to collect it?

JACK. So they say. You never know, mind you. Real chip off the old block. His father was the only man I ever knew answer back to Francis Duggan and get away with it.

CHICK. Francis Duggan?

JACK. Forget it. You never can tell, with VC's and that. There was a corporal in our platoon at Mametz Wood shot down two enemy planes.

138

Single-handed. Greatest act of courage ever I witnessed. He got put up for the VC and was refused.

CHICK. Why?

JACK. They said he was drunk.

CHICK. Worse reason that that—a big fellow with us in France, just before Dunkirk, Keenan they cried him, from Shettleston—he took a pill—box with four Fritzes in it. Took the ammo, the lot. Saved the lives of a dozen men. And he got nothing in the way of medals, because there was no officer there to be a witness. What are you doing?

JACK. Checking the focus on Ibrox. Most important bit of my routine. *(He is at the telescope)* Just in case.

CHICK. In case what?

JACK. Of a raid.

CHICK. Think I'd be here if I thought there was going to be a raid?

JACK. Where are you situated?

CHICK. Up in the church tower. I couldn't give a damn about the war, but I don't want to be up there when we've won. Bloody bells'd drive you crazy. Look, how's about a game of the old darts? Tell you what, we'll get a photo of old Adolf, and use it instead of the board. That'd make his eyebrows twitch. *(Laughs)*

JACK. Think I'd risk that with you about? Next thing you'd be telling the police I was a - -

(The air raid siren: warning. CHICK and JACK stand frozen. Both have tin helmets. JACK trains the telescope. The siren dies away.)

CHICK. Christ, Jack, I'd best get out of here.

JACK. Where to?

CHICK. The church. The church tower. Harry'll need me.

JACK. Let him need you. You cannae go back there now.

CHICK. Why not? You think I'm feared, or something?

JACK. It's too late.

CHICK. What do you mean too late?

JACK. What I say. You wouldnae get out. Martha takes the key with her, when she goes down to the shelter.

CHICK. But we cannae stay up here. You're not intending staying up here, Jack? You're not serious?

JACK. I spend every night up here, sirens or no sirens. Look, what's worrying you? There's warnings every other night. Half of them's practices, to keep the boys on their toes.

CHICK. What if this is different? What if this isnae a warning? What if it's the real thing, Jack, what they've been threatening? Listen, Jack . . .

(Silence.)

JACK. Do you think the enemy's going to fly all the way from Hamburg in a steaming great soup-crate, just to drop one on me? It wouldnae be economic.

CHICK. Come on down, while there's still time. Use the head, Jack.

JACK. You don't understand. I don't desert my post.

CHICK. What do you mean, your post?

JACK. I've got to stay here, to do my bit by him. Sort of like keeping him company. It's the least I can do. If I cannae be out there with him.

CHICK. There's a time and a place for everything. Jack . . .

(The drone of bombers, distant. CHICK rushes to the telescope. JACK puts out the light.)

CHICK. It's them, Jack. This is the night. Where are they? I cannae see a damnt thing.

JACK. You have to lift up the eye-piece first! *(He does so.)*

CHICK. They'll be after the river, so they will. Here

the sky's full of them. In their hundreds, their droves. Have a look for yourself . . . I hope we're prepared, I only hope we're prepared.

JACK. *(He takes the telescope)* You're right. This is what they've been threatening . . . Chick, here, there's one caught in the searchlights. But they're coming on, the others. Open up, will you, bloody well open up on them, before it's too late . . . What are you waiting for?

(Suddenly bombs dropping, and explosions. JACK and CHICK hurl themselves to the floor. Then JACK rises and returns to the telescope.)

CHICK. Get down, Jack. You're off your head!

JACK. Leave me alone . . . where are they, there they are . . . Chick, it's the river, the river they're aiming at. There they go. The river and the docks. . . . And Clydebank. . . Clydebank that's getting it . . . And more of them, waves and waves of them, the river . . . the bloody river, it's on fire . . .

CHICK. What can we do?

JACK. If they come any lower we could pelt them with baked-bean cans. And get ourselves a medal. How's about that, eh? The only VC of the war for bringing down an enemy bomber with baked-bean cans!

(The crump of gunfire. Still the dull throb of the bombers.)

Something's gone up, it must be the Polish tanker, the one that was docked. With its oil drums.

CHICK. No, it's the wrong direction.

JACK. It's . . . it's the houses.

CHICK. It cannae be . . .

JACK. It's the houses, the tenements, that's going up. They're bombing the houses. There's folk in those houses, folk like you and me, Chick. There's folk in these houses, leave them alone will you. . . I cannae bear it, the Holy City, it's a mass of flames, the place is going up in smoke . . . The

Holy City, it's on fire, it's an inferno. I cannae
stand it . . . Christ, can you not do something
. . . can you not prevent it . . . it's Armageddon . . .

(There is a scream of falling bombs.)

CHICK. *(Shrieks)* Get down!

*(CHICK hurls himself at JACK, and they fall
to the floor. Simultaneously, an explosion.
As they lie there, a spot comes up on MARTHA
in her rocking-chair.*

*The bombers, receding now. They get to their
feet and go to the skylight. Outside, a red glow;
The bombers have gone. MARTHA rocks in her
chair. The curtain comes down as the All Clear
sounds.)*

END OF ACT TWO

Lights up on MARTHA's *room.* MARTHA *enters from the kitchen, crosses to the budgie's cage.*

MARTHA. I see the Reverend's bike's down there.
  So he must still be through by, with Amie.
  Wonder if the boys have let his tyres down again,
  Not much the power of prayer can do about that.
  Here, I'll change your water for you, in case I
  forget.

(As she opens the cage:)

It's going to rain, son . . . I feel it . . . in my
  bones. My legs is like . . . animated barometers,
  so they are.

*(She takes the saucer. Instead of going to the
  kitchen, she crosses to the wall dividing her
  room from* AMIE's. *She listens. Sits chair left.)*

Aye, she'll be on about here bells, again . . .

(Pause, then:)

They fair talk the hind legs off one another,
  once they get started!

(She shakes her head, exits to the kitchen.

The lights change: AMIE's *room.* AMIE *and*
  REV. MacWHURRIE. *He is standing.*

MacWHURRIE. I'm afraid that's the decision of the
  meeting, Amie.

AMIE. Miss Cameron donated her money for a
  carillon of bells.

MacWHURRIE. You sound as though you thought the
  fabric fund was unchristian. It's our daily bread,
  Amie. It's necessary for the structure of the kirk.

AMIE. Don't I know it. We hear of nothing else
  every Sabbath, in your intimations. Fabric fund,
  dry rot fund, pound thermometer, and so on.
  This was a heaven-sent opportunity to do something
  new, something fresh and original, for the delight

143

of the people, not just members but outsiders, a carillon of bells, to the glory of God. And what do you do? Turn it down? How churlish can you get?

MacWHURRIE. I don't see that we're necessarily in a position to judge what's to the glory of God and what isn't.

AMIE. I take strong exception to that.

MacWHURRIE. There are more ways of extolling the Lord than ringing bells.

AMIE. Bells. To call His children to worship. What could be better, tell me? What better purpose for a bequest? When the old lady herself wanted it that way? Why should you and your snooty young elders turn down her gift? From what you've told me, it'll be a miracle if the church ever has a carillon of bells.

MacWHURRIE. If we were to put a carillon of bells into that tower, with the dry rot and the structure in the state it is, it'd take an even greater miracle to keep them suspended. The Almighty would have to exert a stronger force than that of gravity.

AMIE. That's taking the Lord's name in vain, John MacWhurrie, so it is. That's bordering on . . .

MacWHURRIE. If those bells were to be installed, the congregation would have to be milked dry, to pay for virtually a new belfry. Think that over, before you come to a final conclusion.

AMIE. I see.

MacWHURRIE. We had many factors to consider, at last night's meeting. That was one of them. It was felt that we could not, with a clear conscience, accept a gift which might admittedly be a joy in itself, but which would by its very nature become a dead weight round our necks. An extra material and financial responsibility.

AMIE. I still think there's a selfishness in—

MacWHURRIE. I see no selfishness on our part, Amie.

AMIE.   But you do on mine, is that it?

MacWHURRIE.   Amie, I know that, well, what you
think of the dull routine functions of church
maintenance and so forth, I appreciate that. But
there are many ways of pleasing the Lord, and of
making His house habitable. Would you not be
prepared to consider giving a gift in another form?

AMIE.   Another form?

MacWHURRIE.   For another purpose. Towards the
general upkeep costs.

AMIE.   I wouldn't consider it. I wouldn't for a moment
entertain the notion. This was to have been in
memory to my mother, as I couldn't afford
enough myself for a stained glass window. How
could I dream of something less . . . well . . . less. . .

MacWHURRIE.   Ostentatious?

AMIE.   I shall take this to the kirk session. I shall take
it to the Presbytery. I have never been so insulted.
The General Assembly will hear of this.

MacWHURRIE.   Well, you'll have a weary wait. They
won't be meeting for another eleven months. Let's
hope this has blown over, and we've both forgotten
all about it by then.

AMIE.   You've spoken to me in a way no minister has a
right to.

MacWHURRIE.   We're not all saints, I'm afraid.

AMIE.   I deplore your conduct.

MacWHURRIE.   Believe you me, your point of view was
not unrepresented. There was a long argument,
there was a lot of hot air and a lot of cold water
poured on things, there were suggestions and
counter-suggestions. But it was thrashed out. I
apologise, as I say, for any rudeness to yourself.

AMIE.   Changed your tune, haven't you. As soon as you
were threatened.

MacWHURRIE.   I'm sorry you won't at least ponder my
suggestion that your own gift, your very generous
and very kind gift, could be given under slightly

different terms from those which you had until now envisaged. This, both as your friend and as your parish minister, I regret. But I assure you, I appreciate your feelings.

AMIE. Have you quite finished?

MacWHURRIE. Yes, thank you.

AMIE. I haven't then. You come insinuating yourself in here, thinking because you're the parish minister, high and mighty, God's representative with your airs and graces and your university degree . . .

MacWHURRIE. *(Holds up his hand)* I have no degree, Amie, you can't accuse me of that.

AMIE. Then you damned well ought to have. A man in your position. That's the trouble. Have you visited the English cathedrals, and listened to their peals, to the changes being rung, to their carillons? Don't you realise how essential these things are to worship? To God's glory?

MacWHURRIE. I wonder if it isn't your denomination you ought to change, Amie, rather than your will.

AMIE. How dare you . . . Your father would have been ashamed of you. You have come here . . .

MacWHURRIE. I shall not stand upon the order of my going. I'm genuinely sorry to have distressed you.

AMIE. It's your own cause you have hurt. You've cost your church, your precious church, you have cost it my contribution. My widow's mite.

MacWHURRIE. My church, perhaps. But I hope not The Church.

AMIE. Yes. The Church. Nothing of mine will go to The Church, after what has passed between us.

MacWHURRIE. I am sorry. Deeply sorry.

(He is at the door. A pause.)

AMIE. Have you no final suggestion?

MacWHURRIE. I am sorely tempted.

(A slight pause.)

AMIE. Well?

MacWHURRIE.   I can only suggest you donate a
   carillon of bells to the Cat and Dog Home.

   *(He exits. She is speechless. Suddenly she turns,
   strides to the flowers, lifts them from their bowl,
   and hurls them to the floor. Then she controls
   herself.)*

AMIE.   To think . . . all those books . . . I'd laid out for
   him . . . To think I . . . I wish I'd really had money
   coming . . . *(Catches herself out)* . . . real money
   that is . . . So that I could have deprived him of it.

   *(She dabs her eyes, puts her handkerchief in her
   sleeve.)*

   And they don't seem to have jumbles now . . . not
   that I could bear . . .

   *(She opens a cupboard, revealing piles of books.
   She sees one, lifts it out . . . a heavy family Bible.)*

   He could have had that . . . for his pulpit . . . or the
   Bible Class maybe . . . But what can I . . . now
   that . . .

   (As she opens the Bible, scans the family tree:)

   There they are . . . look at them . . . weaklings . . .
   poor stock . . . Uncle Lloyd, the money that man
   gambled away . . . They threw it away . . . or lost
   it . . . When it might have come to me . . . I might
   have been sitting pretty . . . living in . . . *(She sighs
   deeply.)* What's the point, I can't change it now . . .
   But they're all dead to me, these names . . . I don't
   know that I even want them . . . But how . . . ?
   Who . . . ? *(She looks up)* I wonder . . . if maybe. . .
   I mean it isn't the sort of thing you can throw
   out . . .

   (AMIE *takes the Bible, dusts it lightly, goes to the
   door, exits.*

   A moment later we hear her knocking on
   MARTHA's *door.*

   The lights change.

   MARTHA *comes from the kitchen. She answers
   the door.)*

147

MARTHA. Who is it?

AMIE. *(Off)* It's me.

MARTHA. It's yourself! What can I do for *you?*

AMIE. Hello, Martha. How are you?

MARTHA. What's this you've got?

AMIE. Oh, I just happened to have it with me.

MARTHA. You might as well get whatever it is off your chest. Yes, come in and sit down.

AMIE. Thanks, but I'll stay standing. My hip, you know.

MARTHA. Been giving you trouble again?

AMIE. It comes and goes. *(Pause)* I've just had Mr. MacWhurrie in to see me.

MARTHA. Is that a fact. Was it him gave you that?

AMIE. No, it's our old family Bible. Not my direct line, but through my step-mother. You know. No, you see, Martha . . . well, mind I mentioned to you about the prospect of the bells. . .

MARTHA. What was that again?

AMIE. How there was the money I couldn't touch. But that I could leave. For a memorial to my mother, of some kind. Well anyway it's a long story. But the long and the short of it is that Mr. MacWhurrie, after stringing me along, leading me up the garden path, has said he doesn't want my gift. What do you make of that?

MARTHA. Doesn't sound like him to me.

AMIE. Well, that's what he said. Between you and me, I wouldn't want it to go any further, he was extremely abrupt. Almost foul-mouthed, for one of his calling. I must admit I got a bit roused myself.

MARTHA. *(Aside)* You're telling me!

AMIE. I beg pardon?

MARTHA. You're not thinking of leaving me a legacy,

are you? I could take it off your hands straight
away, so as it wouldn't be a worry to you.

AMIE.   Scarcely that. No, the thing is, remember my
nephew Donald, well he's meant to be coming to
uplift some books I've kept for him. Specially for
him and his fiancée, charming girl. Well you see,
one of my books is this Bible. And it would be a
waste on him. A mere lad. So I wondered where it
might find a good home. And I thought. . .

MARTHA.   You thought of me.

AMIE.   No, I thought of Mr. MacWhurrie.

MARTHA.   Is that not a bit like coals to Newcastle?

AMIE.   Not a bit of it. Man in his position can't have
too many. But now, you see, that he's adopted
this strange attitude, I couldn't bring myself to . . .
you see the difficulty, Martha?

MARTHA.   You thought I might have a good home for
it?

AMIE.   That's right. You're so understanding.

MARTHA.   Do I get pink stamps with it?

AMIE.   It isn't just it. There's others you could have too.
There's the lives of the Saints. And a lovely wee
series 'Heroes of the Covenant'—you know, men
like Guthrie of Fenwick . . .

MARTHA.   How big's your wee series?

AMIE.   You could have as many as you like. Poets too.
Some of them leather-bound.

MARTHA.   You don't fancy I'd read them? Or the wee
fellow there? Can you see him getting stuck into
Robbie Burns?

AMIE.   But I've no storage space . . . no room . . . And
when the time comes for me to move . . . *(She
looks round)* You've . . . up there . . .

MARTHA.   You'd be as good storing them in a goldfish
bowl.

AMIE.   Just this one, meantime . . . You've no idea how
I'd . . . how I'd appreciate it . . .

MARTHA.   Goodsakes, I'd never get it up the stair.

(AMIE *makes for the attic.*)

AMIE.   No trouble . . . I don't mind . . .

MARTHA.   I thought your hip was bad?

AMIE.   As I said, it comes and goes.

MARTHA.   So I see. Oh all right, leave it up there . . . if it'll please you.

AMIE.   It'll be . . . a great load off my mind.

(AMIE *is in the attic. She screws up her face, sniffs the air, touches a surface, rubs the dust from her fingers.*)

MARTHA.   I'm sure it will. Well, it'll do no harm up there. So long as you don't expect me to clamber up every night and say my portion. *(Pause)* Are you all right?

(AMIE *has been examining the telescope.*)

AMIE.   Yes, why?

MARTHA.   I thought maybe . . . an Oliphant had got you. Never mind, I'm sure there's no Oliphants up there. If there were, they'd be down on us like a ton of bricks.

AMIE.   I'm sorry, I couldn't quite catch that.

MARTHA.   Don't worry, you weren't meant to.

AMIE.   Will I . . . lay it down . . . by the window?

MARTHA.   Lay it down anywhere you want.

AMIE.   *(Blowing some dust away)* Yes . . .

(*Having dusted a space for the Bible, she leaves it, and starts coming down.*)

Thanks, Martha . . . It's none too dry up there. Do you know that?

MARTHA.   You don't tell me!

AMIE.   Will you be all right . . . I mean . . .

MARTHA.   I've a big umbrella.

AMIE. I'm . . . being serious, Martha.

MARTHA. Oh, I see.

AMIE. Sometimes, I just don't know . . . how to take
you. Neither I do.

MARTHA. I'm sometimes not too sure how to take
myself!

(AMIE *laughs. Then the laugh freezes.*)

AMIE. Those workmen, Martha . . . they were typical,
weren't they?

MARTHA. Typical, in what way?

AMIE. Always eating, never getting on with the job.
And the cheek of them. At least the older one. The
young lad was dumb insolence. Not that I suppose
he'd the intelligence to be otherwise. What sort of
job did they do?

MARTHA. You don't suppose I went out on my hands
and knees to have a look, do you?

AMIE. That's what I mean. We're at their mercy. No
way of checking up. You have to . . . take it on
trust. Till one night the roof comes in.

MARTHA. You're cheery.

AMIE. And petty pilfering. There's no sense of . . .
decency, nowadays. Or responsibility. It's every
man for himself. Or rely on the State. That's the
easy way, isn't it. When I was a girl there was no
easy way. Take my Uncle Lloyd, a self-made man
if ever there was one. Only he . . .

MARTHA. He what?

AMIE. He . . . lost it . . . eventually . . . He was . . .
killed in an accident and wasn't insured . . . Do you
know, when I asked those workmen . . . *workmen,*
that's a lie, for a start . . . when I asked if they'd
seen Sammy, they laughed. In my face. *(Pause)*
You haven't seen him around, have you?

MARTHA. Seen him? I haven't even smelt him.

AMIE. What!

MARTHA. It's ... only an expression ... don't get all
touchy ...

AMIE. I'm ... sorry.

(Pause.)

MARTHA. Funny, isn't it ... you and me, living
through the wall all that time, yet seeing so little
of one another.

AMIE. Time flies, doesn't it. I suppose that's life. Not
that we've ... a great deal in common, I suppose ...

MARTHA. Is there any word? About your move?

AMIE. It's taking longer than I expected. If it isn't
through by the winter, I might spend a few weeks
with my sister.

MARTHA. Is she still ... out there?

AMIE. Didn't I tell you? She's back. The climate didn't
agree with her.

MARTHA. You'll ... let me know, won't you ...
before you go ...

AMIE. Of course, why?

MARTHA. I wouldn't want to find out you'd gone.
Without knowing, that is. After you'd been ...
through the wall ... all that time. To wake up one
morning, and discover you weren't there ... any
longer. *(Pause)* It's funny ... the thought of ...
someone else, through there ... I wonder who it'll
be.

AMIE. There's one thing it won't be. Pakistanis.

MARTHA. What's wrong with the Pakis? I'd rather
have the Pakis than ... the likes of Francis
Duggan.

(Pause.)

AMIE. How ... has your own leg been, Martha?

MARTHA. It makes the stairs murder, otherwise I can
thole it not too bad.

(Pause.)

152

AMIE. Is there . . . anything I can get you? Or . . . do for you?

MARTHA. Aye, a colour tellie.

AMIE. No, I mean . . . *(And she laughs, nervously)* I didn't mean . . . Are you sure, Martha? From the shops, I meant.

MARTHA. Positive, thanks.

AMIE. I'd have said to come in and watch mine. It's not colour . . . just the set, I mean . . . Only there's something the matter with it. It's been nothing but trouble, from the outset. I thought it had sorted itself, but it's gone again. It coincided with those workmen, come to think of it. I wouldn't be surprised if they tampered with the aerial.

MARTHA. Probably pinched it.

AMIE. *(Looks at her watch)* My, is that the time! I really must go, I hadn't realised . . . I've kept you long enough . . . I'm sure you've plenty to do, without me—

(A knock on the door.)

MARTHA. Yes?

ELLEN. It's Ellen.

MARTHA. Come in, dear.

AMIE. I was just . . . going . . .

(ELLEN *comes in.*

AMIE *is sidling past her, towards the door.)*

MARTHA. Amie, this is Ellen. She's a great comfort to me. Ellen, this is Miss Wilkie.

(AMIE *gives an exaggerated smile.* ELLEN *nods, slightly stiffly.)*

ELLEN. Pleased to meet you. You're across the stair?

AMIE. Through the wall, that's right. Across the . . . landing.

(Embarrassed pause. Broken by:)

153

MARTHA. Won't you stay for a cup of tea? Ellen'll
make one for us.

AMIE. No . . . really, thanks . . . I really was on the
point of . . . anyway, I didn't realise . . . you were
expecting visitors . . .

MARTHA. Ellen's not visitors.

AMIE. All the same . . . I've left the gas on a low
peep . . . You never know, do you, since all those
strikes started . . . bringing the country to its knees,
if you ask me . . . *(To* ELLEN) Nice meeting you. . .
(To MARTHA) If you're sure there's . . . nothing. . .?

(MARTHA *shakes her head.* AMIE *goes to the
door.)*

Thanks again for . . . you-know-what. Cheery-bye.

MARTHA. Cheerio.

(AMIE *exits.*

MARTHA *and* ELLEN *exchange a look.)*

ELLEN. The times she's passed me on the stair . . .
looked right through me. Go and see what she's
brought me.

(ELLEN *looks puzzled, goes and looks. She sees
the Bible* AMIE *has left.)*

Do you mean the Bible!

MARTHA. Yes.

ELLEN. Is she trying to convert you?

MARTHA. No. She's just found out the bin-men don't
take Bibles. *(Pause)* Still, it's not likely to be in my
road, up there.

(ELLEN *comes back to her.*

In preparation for the next scene, AMIE *enters her
room, finds notepaper, starts writing a letter.)*

ELLEN. Are you ready for a cup of tea?

MARTHA. *(Shakes her head)* Would you like one?

ELLEN. No, thanks. I just called in, in passing. I've
spoken with the factor.

MARTHA. Ellen!

ELLEN. Only about the roof. Nothing else. Not
threatening, anything like that. I simply had a chat.
To ask him to make sure these men did a proper
job. Not only for your sake, but for the good of
his own property.

MARTHA. How often do I have to tell you? It's no
good. They'll be knocking it down, soon. Why
should they—?

ELLEN. They still must make it habitable.

MARTHA. I hope you haven't got me out in the street,
Ellen. Surrounded by my wee bit sticks, here. I
appreciate what you're doing, Ellen . . . but there's
different ways of going about it. How often have I
tried to tell you? They work by their own book of
rules. Not yours. Like Francis Duggan.

ELLEN. I asked the factor to come round.

MARTHA. He's been round.

ELLEN. While it was raining?

MARTHA. No, he always manages to switch that off,
when he reaches the end of the street. They've
that taped too, you know.

ELLEN. Quite unofficially, Martha . . . I asked him to
come round, to see the premises. Some day, it was
raining. All I said to him. . . was, if when he saw
the rain, he honestly thought nothing needed done,
I'd leave it at that. I said I'd leave it entirely to his
own judgment. I meant his conscience, but I
didn't say that. He agreed. To see the back of me,
I suppose. But he said he'd come. To see what it
was like upstairs, when it was actually raining.
When he sees the rain coming in your roof, he will
do something. He'll tell the landlord . . .

MARTHA. That's what I told you—he'd tell the landlord.

ELLEN. And the landlord will see to repairs. He'll
appreciate when the factor tells him how bad the
situation really is, from your point of view. Believe
me, it's all for the best.

MARTHA. Meet him before he comes, will you. Please don't
let him come here alone. You must meet him before-

hand, so as to be sure and come with him. I need
you with me, honest to God I do, Ellen. Don't think
I'm not grateful, it's just that I'm scared ... by it all ...
he really will come, will he? If you phone him?

ELLEN. He'll come. And I'll be with him. You won't be
alone with him. We'll both come, if need be
tomorrow.

MARTHA. You really think something'll be done?

ELLEN. I think so.

MARTHA. I'm grateful to you, lass. Lord knows, I am.
It's good of you.

ELLEN. What was the name you mentioned? Francis
something—a wee while ago, it was. I've never
heard of him.

MARTHA. Och, that's going back years. Mind I told
you I didn't always live here, I started off on the
south side, in Govan? Well, I lived with my
brothers Tommy and wee Alex—he was the
youngest. And three closes up was big Francis
Duggan. If you saw him coming at you, you dived
under the nearest car. Well, one night wee Alex's
in himself, and there comes a banging at the door.
So he goes and yells 'Who is it?' And a voice said
'It's Tommy. Let me in.' So Alex opened the door,
and there was Tommy, with his face slashed to bits
and the blood running down his jacket. And wee
Alex says 'Who done that to you Tommy? Tell me
who done it and I'll get him. I'll kill him,' and
Tommy says 'Just get a cloth, for my face.' But
Alex keeps jouking up and down saying, 'Tell us
who done it, I'll murder him, I'll melt him. . .' So
Tommy leans forward, with what's left of his face,
the blood streaming off him, and he says 'If you
must know, it was Big Francis Duggan.' And wee
Alex stands stock still. And he says in a kind of a
whisper, 'Aw Tommy, you must've said something
for to offend him.' There you are, that was Big
Francis Duggan. If I'd a tame one of him, not all
the landlords in Glasgow could put me off my
meat. Well, it's cheered me up a bit telling you
that.

156

ELLEN. Thanks, Martha. I'm sure things'll turn out all
right. For you and the wee fellow in the cage there.
And if I should come across any Francis Duggans,
I'll tame them and bring them back with me!

MARTHA. I'm sure you could at that, lassie. I wouldn't
put it past you, despite you're such a slim-made
bit thing . . . Here, don't forget your handbag.

(MARTHA shows ELLEN to the door.

*AMIE rises from writing her letter. She glances over
it.)*

AMIE. *(Reading aloud)* 'The bring-and-buy has been
brought forward to the Wednesday of next week,
not the best of nights but there it is. So I will not
be "at home" on that evening just in case you
thought of calling them, with Gloria. For your
information, I have been through the books again
with a fine-tooth comb, weeding out the ones of
lesser interest. Saving the pick, especially those
with the leather covers, you never know where
value may lie. The sooner these are uplifted, the
better. Storage being what it is, and my removal
being imminent. *(She turns the page)* Feel free to
call at any time, except where indicated above. No
advance warning required. And oblige. Your ever
loving . . . Aunt Amie.'

(Putting the letter in its envelope and sealing it.)

I suppose it had best go first-class. Although it'll
probably take just as long . . . *(And she stamps it)*
I wonder . . . *(She glances across towards
MARTHA's room)* I suppose she'd have said, if
there had been . . . anything. I mean, all she has to
do is ask . . . surely she knows that . . . I'd have
stayed a bit longer, if it hadn't been for that . . .
visitor, of hers. . . A snooty creature, if ever I saw
one. . . Still, I suppose it's none of my business . . .
(Sighs) I know, I'll give myself a treat, for once.
I'll see . . . what's on . . . at the Grosvenor. . .
(Hunts for a paper, finds it) That's what I'll . . .
I wonder if it's "Love Story" . . . "Blood of the
Vampire. . ."! Anyway, I'll risk . . . after all, it's
only once in a blue moon . . . *(She gets her hat and
coat, puts them on)* Oh! I was going to put that

157

advert in. Sammy! That cat's been more trouble since he went away than ever he was when I had him about the place . . . And the price of advertising . . . I think maybe I'll leave it . . . meantime . . . Honestly, when you work it out, I'd be about as cheap getting a replacement!

(AMIE *switches out her room light, exits, locks the door behind her.*

Pause, and up on MARTHA.)

MARTHA. I wish I could give you your freedom, son. But would you really want it? The Outside World's no place for budgies. Mind you, you're a hard wee case, in your own way. No flies on you. Jack would have fancied you, so he would. He never went in for animals after wee Jeannie was poisoned. But I'm sure he'd have had a soft spot for you. There's no need to shout, I've my new aid in. The one the lassie brought me. Kind of her, wasn't it? Just the one thing, if Jack had bought a budgie, it would have been light blue. He'd have flushed you down the lavy. God help you!

(Lights up on the attic.

JACK *combs his hair.)*

JACK. *(Sings)*
There's not a team
Like the Glasgow Rangers
No not one, no not one
The Celtic know all about their troubles
We will fight till the day is done . . .

MARTHA. *(From her chair, calls)* Jack, Chick'll be waiting.

JACK. I'll be right down.

MARTHA. Who are they playing, today?

JACK. Cowdenbeath. Shower of yokels.

MARTHA. Can anything not happen, in the cup?

JACK. Bar miracles.

158

MARTHA. Chick'll be waiting, Jack.

JACK. He'll have to wait fill I've found my bunnet.
(He finds it, puts it on) Mind you, they're not a
patch on the old days. I mind when footballers
were footballers. Every man a prince . . . *(And
as he comes down, he reels the names off
religiously)* Robb, Manderson and McCandless,
Meiklejohn, Dixon and Walls, Archibald, Cunningham,
Henderson, Cairns and Morton . . . *(He blows a
kiss to* MARTHA, *as he goes)*

(JACK *exits.*

MARTHA *shakes her head.)*

MARTHA. Football daft, he was. Not that I blame
him. It was all he had. All that was left for him.
After the War. After what happened. He started
brooding. His grief made him . . . embittered.
He survived, by fits and starts, for a while. But
it got the better of him. Poor Jackie . . . I mind,
years afore, him sailing away to his own War.
From the Broomielaw. The lads in their kilts
and their colours, and us seeing them off . . .
the womenfolk. Their backs erect and proud.
Going to do their bit. And us with our weans in
our arms. It was a clear day, you could see Ben
Lomond and the Cobbler clear as clear . . .
against a blue sky. When the ships sailed away.
And there was lumps in our throats. And the pipes
playing. Precious few of them came back. There
was three from our close, lost. But we never
thought of that, at the time. "Wha saw the forty-
second . . . Wha saw them gang awa. . . " It
wasn't easy for us that were left. Scrubbing to be
done. Bread to win, and a lad to be reared and
fed. And clad, and shod. And no man. It was a
long time, in an empty bed. Since the bands
played, the piper strode the pier, the handker-
chiefs fluttering in the breeze . . . the one you
gave me, Jackie . . . with the flowers on it . . .

Then the wheel turned . . . full circle. For him
and me. All those years later. With the news about
our boy. That he'd been . . . that there was . . .
no hope. I tried to put a good face on it . . .

And the neighbours helped . . . them that were here then. . . But Jack . . . he went clean to pieces afterwards . . . There was . . . nothing I could do about it . . . Nor Chick neither . . .

(Again the lights come up on the attic. This time JACK sits there, head down, CHICK comes in, listens a moment, looks up.)

CHICK. *(Calls)* Jack? *(Pause)* Jack!

(JACK *does not reply.*
CHICK *starts to go to the attic.)*

Come on, Jack. Get a bender on.

JACK. Come on where?

CHICK. The game, where do you think?

JACK. I'm going to no bloody game.

CHICK. Don't be stupid.

MARTHA. Please, Chick . . . don't . . .

CHICK. *(Without turning round at all)* You keep out of it, Martha. *(As she makes to interrupt)* It's the best thing for him.

(MARTHA *makes a helpless gesture, rises painfully and exits to the kitchen. CHICK has ignored her completely.)*

It isn't 'any bloody game', Jack. It could be the League decider. *(As he reaches the attic)* What's up, are you in the huff?

JACK. Do you want me to put one on you?

CHICK. If you did I'd bloody fell you.

JACK. Maybe I'd like that. Then I wouldn't . . . remember . . . I wouldn't have . . . these thoughts . . .

CHICK. *(Gently)* Come on to the game, you don't want to miss this one.

JACK. Just leave us in peace, will you.

CHICK. There's no point brooding. I mean . . . there's no point. It doesn't . . . solve anything. It

160

won't . . . do any good. Either for you, or for
Martha. Don't you see that?

JACK.   If you don't get out of here, I'll break your
bloody neck.

CHICK.   Look, Jack . . . you can't change . . . what's
happened . . . I sympathise with you, God knows
I do . . . But you've a life still to lead . . . staying
up here, and moping . . . that's not going to help
any.

JACK.   Meaning what?

CHICK.   Well it's not going to bring him back, is it?

JACK.   What did you say?

CHICK.   Face facts, Jack. You're not . . . the only
one that lost his boy in the War.

JACK.   Christ, Chick . . .

CHICK.   You're not . . . unique. You go on as if you'd
been . . . singled out, or something. There's
others. In this city. In Europe. Jack, you've got
to see reason. Look, my Bess lost three boys . . .
blown out the bloody skies . . . You don't
imagine it's easy for her, do you? Three, one
after the other. And there's others, in the same
boat. I'm not . . . trying to lessen what's happened
Jack. But you have to go on. Somehow. I
don't know how. But somehow. All I'm doing's
trying to . . . help. Pull yourself together, Jack.
Will you not come to the game?

JACK.   My boy . . . copped his, just before the final
whistle . . . my boy . . . And you stand there, and
talk about . . . going to the game . . . By Christ
. . .

(MARTHA *appears from the kitchen.*)

MARTHA.   Leave him be, Chick.

CHICK.   He won't listen to reason . . .

MARTHA.   Off you go to the game. Thanks for . . .
trying . . .

(CHICK *looks back towards* JACK, *shrugs, is
about to speak to* MARTHA.)

161

On you go, Chick . . . or you'll miss the kick-
off . . .

(CHICK *exits.*
MARTHA *closes the door, glances up, returns
to the foot of the attic stair and stands listening.*)

JACK.   If they'd simply shot him, if it had been clean,
and quick, it mightn't have been so bad. But I
can't bear to think what they did to him. Out
there. And You didn't do anything about it. You.
The Big Referee. Well, did you? No bloody
answer. You let it happen. They took him and
stripped him and put him in a cage, they put
him in a cage under the burning sun, and they . . .
while you sat, up there in your Big Blue Heaven
. . . looking down on Burma . . . you Bastard . . .

MARTHA.   *(Calls up)* Will I not bring you a bite to
eat, Jackie?

JACK.   I've . . . no stomach . . . for it.

MARTHA.   You've got to eat.

JACK.   It's no good. I can't blot it out.

MARTHA.   I know how you feel, but that doesn't - -

JACK.   Leave me in peace, will you?

MARTHA.   Just a bite, Jackie?

JACK.   I said, leave me in peace. Just leave me . . .
in peace . . .

(She exits to the kitchen.
JACK *takes a bottle, pours a whisky, drinks.*)

*(He finishes his drink, pours another, lies down
wearily, the bottle at his side.*

Pause, then he gives a single drawn-out moan.

As the lights change, MARTHA *enters.*

MARTHA *comes in.*)

MARTHA.   *(To budgie)* Gives me a headache, this
weather. Are you all right, son? Nothing to be
scared of. Nothing's going to happen to you.

It'll just be wind and rain. And even if there's
thunder, that's just clouds banging into one
another. Up in the sky. You'll be ready for
another bird-bath by now. I'll just have a wee
sit-down, and then I'll renew your water. I
hope it doesn't thunder, all the same. I don't
mind the thunder, it's the lightning. I mind I
was a wee girl, and I was in the lavvy, across the
back-court, when it came on a sudden thunder-
plump. And I've never been so terrified in my
life. Sat there frozen stiff, till my mammy came
shouting for me. Think she thought I must've
fell through the seat. It makes God awful big
and fearsome, thunder, like the Old Testament.
Tell you what, I could get the attic area fixed
out as a big sort of birdcage for you. With spars
on the window. That'd be the place for you. Not
so cramped as where you are now. Bags of room to
flutter in. You could do your wee nut, so you
could. Aye, that'll be the day. I'll not manage up
those stairs again. Ought to have the whole jing-
bang boarded up. That'd be the best thing. It
was never the same again, son. Without you. For
Jack and me . . . I mind the day the telegram
came. Jack opened it, he never said a word, just
turned white as a sheet, I thought he was going to
faint. And then he said, 'It's bad, Martha.' And I
asked him, was it the boy? And he just nodded.
And I said how bad, was it really bad, was he
wounded? And Jack said to me, to hold on to
something, it was worse than that. And I knew.
Oh, Jackie, Jackie . . .

*(The lights come up on the attic. JACK rises. He
has his darts. He throws them dispiritedly at the
board. He pours a drink, lays the glass down,
takes the darts, throws them again.*

*We are aware, far in the distance, of cheering,
and shouting from the football ground across
the river. Mingled with the shouting: 'Follow,
follow . . .' being sung. Suddenly a roar, as a
goal is scored. JACK downs his drink.*

*The sound of the football crowd mix into those
of a storm: gusts of wind and rain.*

163

The skraiking of a revolving chimneycan.

*The lights on the attic dim. We are left again
with* MARTHA.)

MARTHA.　*(Sings)*
　　　　　'Wha saw the Forty-Second,
　　　　　Wha saw them gang awa,
　　　　　Wha saw the Forty-Second
　　　　　Sailing down the Broomielaw . . .

　　　　　'Wha saw the Forty-Second,
　　　　　Wha saw them sail awa . . .'

(Listening to the chimney-can) I wish whoever's
chimney that is would get their granny sorted. . .

(Sounds of storm, outside.)

If only you'd come back, son, what a hero's
welcome there'd have been. The train arriving at
the Central Station, all the crowds at the barriers,
Jack and me with special tickets. Then out into
Gordon Street, where the band's waiting, all trig
and spruce. Across Hope Street into Waterloo
Street, all the folk cheering and waving flags and
banners and throwing handfuls of confetti. Away
out Argyle Street, past the Kelvin Hall, the band
playing fit to burst. Into Dumbarton Road, the
shops done up, bunting stretched across the street.
Streamers and pennants, the steamers tooting in
the distance. Then swinging round at Merkland
Street, the whole of Partick out to . . . to greet
you . . . son . . . But it wasnae to be, was it . . .

(A distant peal of thunder. She ignores it.)

All the time, you were in your cage. In the cage
where they put you, stripped naked. And they
never opened the cage again . . . Stripped naked,
son . . . and scattered over the globe. I don't belong
here. Not any more. I don't belong anywhere any
more. It's getting cold . . . And the rain . . . don't
let the rain come in on me, before they come. Will
no one ever come?

(Sound of a slate sliding: she starts.)

Oh God . . . please protect me . . . Lord, please
protect me . . . the landlord ought to protect me . . .

will no one come . . . ? Jackie, come down for your
tea. You can't stay up there all night long. Come
down and go to your bed Jackie, for pity's sake . . .
Jackie . . .

*(Sounds of the storm. As she looks up, the lights
come up on the attic. JACK throws two darts,
which stick in the board. He throws a third, which
hits the wall and falls. He steps forward to pick it
up. Doing so, he leans agains the board with his
other hand. He lifts the dart, and stands staring at
it. His expression changes.*

MARTHA, *as though anticipating what he's going
to do, screams:)*

MARTHA. Jackie . . . !

*(Suddenly he drives the dart through his hand,
transfixing it to the board. Simultaneously, a peal
of thunder. MARTHA claps her hands over her ears.
The lights on the attic fade. MARTHA, alone, takes
her hands from her ears. The storm has almost spent
itself.*

She looks up.)

MARTHA. Jackie . . . !

*(Suddenly he drives the dart through his hand,
transfixing it to the board. Simultaneously, a peal
of thunder. MARTHA claps her hands over hands
from her ears. The storm has almost spent itself.
She looks up.)*

I hope no one hurts you, son. That's all. I hope no
one tries to hurt you . . .

If I could just give you your water, that would be
me happy . . .

(She rises, and crosses to the budgie's cage.)

MARTHA. Hold your wheesht, son, there's nothing to
be frightened at. I'm going to give you your water,
if I can manage. . .

(But she loses her balance, and slumps forward.)

I'm sorry, son, I cannae make it . . . it's no use . . .

165

But the least I can do is open your cage. And let
you out. To make sure no one tries to hurt you . . .
I'll set you . . . free . . . son . . .

(With difficulty, she stretches towards the cage.)

I'll open your cage . . . and let you go . . . I don't
want . . . any . . . of . . . them . . . to hurt you . . .

(The budgie chirps and chatters.
The lights on her slowly fade.)

CURTAIN